Out of
Mormonism

A Woman's True Story

Out of
Mormonism

Judy Robertson

BETHANYHOUSE
Minneapolis, Minnesota

Published by Bethany House Publishers
A Ministry of Bethany Fellowship International
11400 Hampshire Avenue South
Bloomington, Minnesota 55438
www.bethanyhouse.com

Printed in the United States of America by
Bethany Press International, Bloomington, Minnesota 55438

Library of Congress Cataloging-in-Publication Data

Robertson, Judy.
    Out of Mormonism : a woman's true story / by Judy Robertson.
       p.   cm.
Rev. ed. of: No regrets. © 1997.
Includes bibliographical references.
    ISBN 0-7642-2604-5 (pbk.)
    1. Church of Jesus Christ of Latter-day Saints—Controversial literature.
2. Robertson, Judy. 3. Ex-church members—Church of Jesus Christ of Latter-day
Saints—Biography. 4. Christian biography—United States. I. Robertson, Judy. No
regrets. II. Title.
    BX8645 .R64   2001
    289.3—dc21   2001002519

acknowledgments

But for the help and encouragement of the following people, this book would not be in your hands today:

To Charles Cook, my first spiritual guide who counseled me when I felt hopeless after leaving the Latter-day Saints Church.

To John Hendee, whose creative ideas sparked the printing of the original Concerned Christians' *Witness to Mormons*.

To the anonymous donor who challenged us to complete it, and to Bill Pinch, the real motivator, who put us on the road to printing *Witness to Mormons*.

To Roy Lawson, who told me, "This is the stuff books are made of," when I wrote letters about our incredible journey on a ministry yacht in the South Pacific.

To Don Cox, who said, "You need to keep writing," when I thought I was wasting time.

To Norm Rohrer, Christian Writers Guild, who gave me permission to say I was a writer as I pecked away on a rusty typewriter on a small island in the South Pacific.

To Donna Goodrich, my first contact with a Christian writers' club, and a continual help in more ways than I can mention.

To Bobbi Preston, whose gentle words and incredibly accurate pen helped me realize "Delete" was the most important key on my computer.

To Joy Moore, who believed in me and whose brainchild, our Tuesday's Children critique group, read and offered invaluable suggestions for every chapter.

To Betty Arthurs, Marsha Crockett, Dorothy Barnes, and Andrea Huelsenbeck, who, along with Joy, make up Tuesday's Children. They are my cheerleaders for whom I can't thank God enough.

To Steve Laube, who, at an American Christian Writers Conference, told me I needed to put my South Pacific book on hold and write this book first. I didn't want to hear this advice, but I'm so grateful I took it. Thanks, Steve.

To Bob Haslam, editor of Light and Life Communications, who saw the potential for this book at Mount Hermon Christian Writers Conference and desired to publish it. Every writer needs a champion; Bob is mine. Thank you, Bob.

To John Van Valin, publisher, who treated me like a professional and walked me through the signing of the contract.

To my children, their spouses, and my mom, who've graciously let me slide with some family traditions and have taken them over. To my grandchildren, who want me to speak to their classes at school and church. I love you all.

Last, but not least, to my husband, Jim, who has been incredibly patient with my many hours sitting in front of the computer, and has put up with many quick-cook meals and a multitude of household projects put on hold. This is *our* story of what God has done in and through us.

To the Lord of my life, who placed it in the heart of each of these servants of His to encourage me.

contents

PART FOUR: MY LIFE AFTER MORMONISM

RESOURCES

mormonism
looks good

1

The Weakness

H OW CAN SUCH GOOD PEOPLE BE WRONG? I thought. *There's gotta be something there. Surely if God designed His church for today's world, it would be like this one.*

Jim's account with Campbell Soup took him to the Arizona farmlands each year from May to the first of July. He needed to be there during potato harvest to oversee grading, loading, and shipping to ensure top quality spuds. Although this was my first time accompanying him with our kids, I heard my husband rave so much about Joe Jackson and his family, I'd gotten sick of it. "Judy, these are the finest people you'll ever meet."

At first, I made serious accusations. "Jim, these people just want your business," I said cynically. "That's why they're being so nice. They're snowing you."

"Judy, how can you say that? They're just sincere, hard-working people."

"Well, I have a funny feeling about them. And what is their religion? Mormon? I've never heard of that before."

"They are totally committed to it. I've never seen anything like it. Everything they do revolves around their church and family."

After a summer of observing this "all-American" family in action, I began to see their appealing qualities, too. *Boy, they really do have something! Certainly something we don't. I want to know more.*

My depleted spiritual life needed to be recharged, especially after a recent incident at our home church in Fayetteville, Arkansas. I guess you could say my spiritual candle was flickering.

At a vacation Bible school planning meeting, I sat with my co-director in her elegant living room. I opened my heart and unfolded what I thought were innovative and fresh ideas for the kids. In the middle of my presentation she interrupted me. "We've never done it this way before, and I don't know who you think you are, trying to change our VBS!" she sputtered, eyes glaring at me. Her words stung and I sat speechless. Unable to go on, I swallowed hard, gathered my things, and left her home like a whipped puppy.

I choked back tears all the way home. Once in our bedroom I lamented, *How could she be so cruel?*

I knew after a good fifteen-minute sob I needed to get my feelings under control fast. The kids would be back soon from their friends' house and Jim home for supper.

After eight years of marriage, Jim's way was to try to "fix" my hurt feelings. He'd say something like "Why didn't you just tell her off?"

But I couldn't bring myself to tell off anyone. So I stuffed it in my hurt-feelings bag never to tell anyone—not even God. I didn't know how to share my hurts with God, and I hadn't studied the Bible enough to know we should "bear one another's burdens."

I'd been a church attendee all my life, listened to lots of sermons, but I didn't know how my faith should work in times of crisis. That's why I looked forward to this family trip and meeting these "fine" people Jim kept telling me about.

A CLOUD OF DUST caught up with Joe Jackson's truck as he skidded to a stop beside the still-turning props of our Twin Comanche airplane. "Hurry up, honey, I want to say hello to Joe."

"Mom, where are the bathrooms? I can't wait any longer." Janet, six, squirmed in the four-seater company plane, struggling with her seatbelt. Our four-year-old son, Steve, squeezed past my seat. He'd already taken care of the no-pot-up-in-the-air business by using the Ziploc bags we'd brought along. Our pediatrician suggested our kids could "bomb the coyotes" while in the air.

We could already smell the dusty Arizona farmland, so different from the lush greenness of our home in Arkansas.

"Jim, are you sure people live here?"

"Don't worry, you'll see. The potato shed is over there." Jim pointed to a long, tin-roofed building with a train car pulled up along one side and several trailer trucks parked on the other. "Queen Creek's down the road. It's just a post office, a few general stores, and the Mormon church. Families live on big ranches spread out all over the desert."

"Welcome, folks. You look like you could use a drink." Joe was the grower Jim bought most of his potatoes from.

That's putting it mildly, I thought. My teeth crunched the dust that stirred from his truck. *This is the hottest air I've ever felt in my life—it's like a blast furnace!* My skin felt gritty. *I think standing under a faucet would be more appropriate!*

THE JACKSON FAMILY put us up in an apartment house they owned right off Main Street, near the center of the city of Mesa. After we had a welcome shower to get the accumulated dust off, they took us out to dinner.

Our kids enjoyed the apartment complex's swimming pool. Across the street from our summer home was a lush green park, and we were only a block away from the gleaming white Mormon temple. Its acres of cool grass, tall palm trees, and sparkling fountains were an oasis in the desert.

They treated us like family, taking us out to eat and to church and to family cookouts. "I'll have to admit, Jim, any people I've ever been around that I've thought were really Christians have these same attributes. They are good, loving, family-oriented people." In no time, I forgot the unpleasant experience with the church member back in Fayetteville.

Jim and I agreed before we married that we would join a "neutral" church if we couldn't agree on his Lutheran background or my Disciples of Christ upbringing. We believed that if our family prayed together we'd stay together.

After hopping from church to church to find our niche, we finally settled on the First Christian Church. I had attended it as a college student at the University of Arkansas.

We jumped right into the activities. Jim was on the church board and eventually became vice chairman. One summer, I co-directed the vacation Bible school. It was during this time I felt the sting of the sharp words of my co-director criticizing my ideas. Even though I attended church regularly, I didn't adequately know how to call on God for my needs. Perhaps you could call me a social Christian.

I never searched the Scriptures I'd learned about, sung about, and heard every Sunday during my entire life. I was president of Christian Youth Fellowship, played piano for Sunday school, attended church camp every summer, and sang in the choir with my mother.

Jim received "proper training," too. Raised in the Lutheran faith, he learned many Scriptures to be able to pass the exam for catechism. "I didn't continue learning Scriptures and eventually forgot all I'd been taught," Jim recalled.

Satan is subtle, catching us in our weakness. Nursing my wounds from the sharp tongue of a less-than-tactful church member, the kids and I traveled with Jim on this fateful trip into the desert of Arizona to buy potatoes. Little did we know this journey would change our lives forever.

2

The Questions

IT SEEMED MOST OF QUEEN CREEK was populated by the Jackson family. "My aunt is postmistress and my uncle is a cattle rancher," Lyn, Joe's sister, told me. "My sister's husband grows potatoes, too." Any number of children from the family were constantly around.

Not only did the family do business together, but they all attended church together. And when Lyn took her kids to Primary, the church's program for elementary-age children, she took ours along, too.

Lyn and her husband, Larry, took us to their church meeting on Sunday. Jim went with Larry to "priesthood" meeting. I wanted to see what the children's Sunday school was like.

"I say these things in the name of Jesus Christ. Amen." A tow-headed three-year-old skipped down from the child-sized podium and marched with arms folded back to his seat next to fifteen other three- and four-year-olds. *How sweet,* I thought. *What a good way to train children to be obedient.*

Our kids joined us walking down the hall from the Sunday school room to the large chapel. Both adults and children were present. It was rather noisy with the crunch of Cheerios from antsy toddlers and fussy babies being jostled and cooed to by family members. I strained to hear the talks of the two lay members whom Lyn said were chosen to speak that day.

But what surprised me was what they referred to as the *sacrament*. Young men, sixteen years old, called priests, read a prayer from a card at the sacrament table, blessing it. Twelve-year-old boys, called *deacons*, passed trays of torn pieces of soft white bread and tiny cups of plain water.

I guess water and bread is just as good a substitute as any for Communion, I thought. *Lots less trouble and mess—especially since all the children take it, too.*

L YN TOOK ME TO SEE the Bishop's Storehouse, the church-run cannery in Mesa, where grapefruit, oranges, and other juices and foods from church-owned produce farms were canned. Members who were on church welfare manned the production line.

The church's Relief Society women donated much of their time there, too. They even sewed underwear and other clothing items for needy church members.

Rows of ladies sat at heavy-duty sewing machines in this huge warehouse. I was impressed. Surely God's church on earth would function in such a way.

When we traveled in our company plane with Joe and Larry, they always bowed their heads in prayer and asked for safety as the engines revved and we waited for clearance to take off. We were constantly impressed by the way they lived out their faith daily—not just on Sundays.

Jim and I didn't try to find a temporary church home to attend while in Mesa. We left that aspect of our lives back in Fayetteville.

We were amazed by the way this family-friendly church operated. Every Mormon church throughout the world uses identical Sunday school material. Uniform lessons were also used in Primary and Relief Society. They even had devotional booklets for the women who were *visiting teachers* and made monthly visits to other ladies assigned to them. No one had to scramble around trying to prepare lessons from scratch. All lessons were prepared and sent out by the hierarchy in Salt Lake City to the various churches. It made a well-oiled operation.

I didn't question this. It seemed a good idea at the time—not like the reinvent-the-wheel kind of work we did each time we taught a lesson at our church.

How comfortable it must be to just follow an already planned program. The brain could rest a bit. I didn't stop to think about the danger in this. I was too naïve, and hungry for something that made sense to me.

It was a far cry from the intellectual atmosphere of our university-town church, where we heard lots of politics and very little Scripture. We were hungry for more solid, biblical messages.

I wasn't close enough to anyone in my home church to reach out when I didn't have a car, and I struggled with loneliness. Jim smoked, I drank coffee, and we had occasional cocktails with friends at Jaycee functions. We weren't straight-laced by any means, but the clean-cut lifestyle of the Mormon families in Queen Creek and Mesa looked mighty appealing. *Surely this is the way life should be,* I thought.

L ARRY, I'VE NOTICED some admirable things about your church. Mind telling me a little about it?" The half-hour drive from Mesa to Queen Creek each day gave Jim a perfect opportunity to learn about this too-good-to-be-true religion. Larry, Joe's brother-in-law, was more than happy to accommodate his captive audience.

I asked my own questions of Lyn and other women in their family. "Why do Mormons fast the first Sunday of every month?"

"We give the money we would have used for food to support the needy in our church. It's our welfare system," Lyn responded. "That way we don't depend on the government. We take care of our own."

It seemed like a great idea to me to take care of our own. Why didn't our church do that? Why were we so inefficient and uncaring for our own people? These questions disturbed me. The Mormon way looked more and more appealing.

Jim and I didn't have a great deal of time to discuss these things with each other, because he worked from sunup to sundown in the potato fields. Harvest time drained his energy. But another harvest was about to occur. We were fertile soil for the slick package of Mormonism.

Tempter's Snare

Y OU KNOW, WE CAN ANSWER *some* of your questions, Jim," Larry said, "but why don't you and Judy come over and have dinner with us? We'll have someone here who can answer *all* your questions."

"Okay, Larry, we will." We had no reason to suspect anything other than an informative evening of learning about the history and inside working of the Mormon Church.

Jim and I sank down in the soft pillows on Larry and Lyn's comfortable couch. Children's pictures hung on the huge family room wall. We felt relaxed in our friends' home.

Two men in dark pants, white shirts, conservative ties, and black name tags came after dinner. Jim knew one of them as part owner of a local car agency. "I'm Elder Wilson, Jim and Judy, and this is my partner, Elder White." I would have preferred first names, but *Elder* was what they wanted to be called.

The two men were amiable, warm, and knowledgeable—full of facts about the origin of Mormonism and how it functions today. But we weren't expecting such a formal presentation complete with flannelgraph story. "We have more to show you, Jim and Judy," Elder Wilson said. "Can we come back next Thursday evening?"

"I'm very tired after working out at Queen Creek," Jim answered. "But I suppose so. We do have lots more questions."

After the first lesson, Jim and I went back to the apartment. I felt numb and shocked. Jim was exhausted from his day in the fields, and surprised, too, at the way the evening went. We had expected an informal evening.

Obviously a well-rehearsed presentation, it was anything but informal. Charts flowed, smoothly depicting Joseph Smith's first vision and the progression of the "authority" in the church. And we were put on the spot, a place we were unprepared to be. The elders asked us questions that had only one answer, like "Do you feel that all churches can be teaching the truth, *even* when they teach conflicting ideas?"

Though we felt unnerved, we didn't review what they'd told us about the beginning of Mormonism in 1820. Especially the bizarre story about their founder Joseph Smith and how he saw a vision of angel-like beings as a fourteen-year-old boy. The youth was alone in a grove of trees, the elders said, when he had this vision. Elder White quoted Joseph as saying, "One of them spake unto me, calling me by name, and said, pointing to the other, 'This is My Beloved Son. Hear Him!' . . . I asked the personages who stood above me in the light, which of all the sects was right."

Present-day prophets, said the two, were the Father and

the Son—two separate beings. Joseph was quoted as saying, "I was answered that I must join none of them, for they were all wrong; and the personage who addressed me said that all their creeds were an abomination in his sight; that those professors were all corrupt."

The missionaries' stories failed to impress us, but the Mormon lifestyle did. It seemed impeccable. At a vulnerable time in our lives, we were drawn to their exemplary family. We thought there must be more to their religion than just a weird story. "It can't hurt to listen," Jim reasoned. "Besides, we don't want to offend them. They treat us like family."

"We'll have the lessons every night instead of once a week," Elder White told us. "You two will be leaving for Arkansas after the potato harvest, so we need to take advantage of what time we have left."

With our skimpy knowledge of the Bible, we accepted, unchallenged, their explanation for certain Scriptures. We swallowed the alluring bait—hook, line, and sinker.

After about the fourth lesson, we were asked, "Would you like to set a date to be baptized into the Mormon Church? Many Mormons in Mesa will be praying for your answer. You can tell us what you've decided on Friday night."

We hadn't been shopping for another religion, and yet a sense of urgency pervaded our new friends' tone.

The next day I received phone calls at the apartment during which Mormons in Mesa and Queen Creek said, "I'm praying for you to have the right answer tonight at six." I felt I was in a pressure cooker with the fire on full blast.

That evening we found ourselves saying yes to a question

we had never asked. And the following week, in a Mormon ward building in Apache Junction, Arizona, the entire extended Jackson family watched as we entered the tainted waters of Mormonism that would stain our entire lives.

4

Strong Delusion

BEFORE WE RETURNED to Arkansas, we accompanied the Jackson family to their home in Salt Lake City for a visit. We toured all the historical sites relative to the Mormon faith. This trip locked us in to Mormondom. It was awe-inspiring to see the way the "saints" had struggled across the plains in crude handcarts and carved a virtual garden out of salt-laden desert plains.

"This is where Brigham Young stopped the wagon train, looked over the valley, and said, 'This is the place.'" Larry proudly showed us the monument to that moment in the history of Mormonism. "It was 1847 when President Young led the first pioneer company of 143 men, three women, and two children to the Salt Lake Valley. He recognized the land as the future home of the saints from having seen it in a vision." The monument sat overlooking the outskirts of the lush green Salt Lake Valley.

Saints, I discovered, was short for *Latter-day Saints.* Whenever the LDS Church was mentioned, it was never "our church," to distinguish it from other churches, but "the church," as though it were the one and only—and to the Latter-day Saints, it is the one and only true church. I also discovered that we would be called Brother and Sister Robertson, and we were to do the same with others. It felt strange to call another by a last name rather than a first—and precede it by "Brother" or "Sister." Indeed, I felt I had taken on a new life, but it didn't quite fit.

"This was nothing but desert wasteland when the saints arrived here," Larry told us. "But they began farming this land right away and planted the trees and made this valley blossom like a rose."

I was amazed. These rugged individuals—saints—had accomplished an incredible feat. The Salt Lake Valley had been dead and barren. They had worked hard cultivating and farming under the direction of the second president and prophet of the church, Brigham Young.

We were told an amazing story about a swarm of locusts that threatened to eat up their crops, but a flock of sea gulls flew down and devoured them, saving the crop. There is even a monument to the gulls on Temple Square.

Larry drove us around Temple Square, where the Beehive House was located and where Young's many wives lived. *Beehive* became the state logo to describe the industrious saints who settled there. "Put your shoulder to the wheel; push along,"[1] a favorite hymn of the LDS people, describes not only their work ethic but also their spiritual ethic. *Commendable,* I thought.

The visitors center and the grand tabernacle, where the famous Mormon Tabernacle Choir rehearsed and recorded its majestic choral work, capped off our tour. The imposing nature of it all made me feel like a child viewing the Grand Canyon or Niagara Falls for the first time. I had never seen anything to compare with it. *Surely these are God's people,* I thought.

We weren't allowed in the temple itself, not yet anyway. We would have to go through a year proving ourselves worthy members. After a year's probation, we would have an extensive and personal interview with high officials of the church. They would determine our worthiness, and we would be given a *temple recommend*—a card that looked like a driver's license and stated we had been found worthy to enter the temple.

Duly impressed with the trappings of Mormonism, I felt sure this was the only true church. The fruit of its beauty surrounded me, and the fruit looked luscious. We were *chosen* people, part of the elect, baptized by those who held the "proper authority" handed down by Jesus Christ himself. My eyes were blinded by the shiny package of a church whose members seemed to be on the inside track with God, and I would begin running with them.

Part Two

My Life As a Mormon Woman

5

Fruitless Seeds of Darkness

THE WARMTH OF THE ARIZONA SUNSHINE would soon fade with the foreboding clouds that lay ahead of us at home in Arkansas. Somehow it didn't seem so much like home anymore. We had laid aside all that had previously been important to us and had taken on the shroud of Mormonism.

We renounced all the vices forbidden in the Word of Wisdom—drinking coffee, tea, or alcohol, and Jim gave up smoking. This advice was from the *Doctrine and Covenants*, one of the four books of Mormon scripture. We had to "repent" of these things. It was a measuring rod to determine in part our personal worthiness to become members.

An avid coffee drinker, this was no easy abstinence for me. A cup of coffee had been a part of my morning ritual for all my adult life. My lower intestine rebelled, and I had some problems off and on for three months. I was miserable. But I knew I must keep the Word of Wisdom to be able to enter the temple. It was part of "enduring to the end."

No longer would we attend First Christian Church, where family and friends worshiped at its lovely historic setting on Dickson Street in Fayetteville, Arkansas. The friendships we enjoyed in Jaycees and Jaycettes wouldn't fit in with our new Mormon lifestyle either. Even family gatherings would become strained.

I never thought about how uncomfortable this would make our family. Being part of the "only true church," we had been baptized by one who held the priesthood, the only ones with the proper authority to perform this ordinance. The baptisms in our previous churches were invalid because they had not been performed by the *holy Melchizedek priesthood*. I felt superior.

"We can't drink coffee or tea any longer. It's an ordinance of the church," I told my mom and dad. They were silent. They simply didn't know what to make of this change that had taken place in me.

Our own marriage vows would have to be performed again in the temple, this time for "time and all eternity." Our children would be *sealed* to us, also, for eternity. But this could not happen for a year. We would have to be determined worthy at the end of our probationary time and at the conclusion of an interview with church authorities.

Our first job would be to find a local congregation, if there was one. We looked in the Yellow Pages, and sure enough, Mormons had settled here. Jim called the number listed. "Hello, this is Jim Robertson. My wife, Judy, and I recently joined the LDS Church, and we were wondering where the church building is and when the services are held."

"Why yes, Jim, this is Brother Anderson. I'm so happy you called." That afternoon we drove to the address Brother Anderson had given us, only to find a small, shabby building on College Avenue in Fayetteville. Formerly a grocery store, the members had covered the large front plate-glass window with beige draperies. It was a one-room building and a far cry from the well-constructed and well-appointed Disciples of Christ church we had attended. I was disappointed. After seeing the magnificent buildings in Salt Lake City, this one didn't fit my expectations.

A part of me shut down that day. The part that traveled in the tradition given me by my parents and grandparents, whose faith was in the God of the Bible. I silently said good-bye to friends as well as family who weren't Mormon.

I also said good-bye to the little girl who sang faithfully in the church choir and often accompanied songs for Sunday school on the piano. The music in me ceased. I no longer hummed the melodies of the words that told of the faith of saints from hundreds of years before us. I learned new songs.

The Latter-day Saints hymnal contained songs I had never heard before: "We Thank Thee, O God, for a Prophet," "Come, Come, Ye Saints," and "O My Father[1]"— in which one verse assumed there was a heavenly mother: "Truth is reason, truth eternal, tells me I've a mother there." These replaced the spontaneous words that came into my mind from years of Sunday school, church camp, and Christian Youth Fellowship.

As I joined the "only true church," my creativity and spontaneity that had been forged in my inmost being seemed to dry up inside me. I sang to a god with flesh and bone, who had a wife and spawned millions of spirit babies. I thought I had been born again as one of them. Instead, I entered a pit of darkness where the seed of spirituality, planted in me by faithful saints and parents in the Christian church where I grew up, died. And now I would reap the fruitless seeds of darkness.

6

Dead Works

I BEGAN ACCOMPANYING on the piano the dozen or so children attending Sunday school in this small branch of the LDS Church. The tiny storage room barely had room for the piano, folding chairs, and a podium, where children learned as soon as they could talk to "bear their testimony" of the truthfulness of the *gospel*.

Their testimonies went something like this: "I believe Joseph Smith is a prophet of God, that Spencer Kimball is a prophet of God, and that this is the only true church. I love my mommy and daddy, my sisters and brothers, and I say these things in the name of Jesus Christ, Amen."

Our own children would spend their formative years hearing about stoic pioneers—the early LDS members who crossed the plains in search of a place to live out their lives the Mormon way without persecution. They would no longer learn Bible verses in Sunday school, but lessons prepared by the hierarchy in Salt Lake City.

I partnered with a faithful Mormon woman calling on a

list of ladies we were to see every month. We were called *visiting teachers*. We were supposed to discreetly find out why they hadn't been attending, give a devotional from the visiting teachers manual, and write up a report on the status of the family. I dreaded this once-a-month ritual. I felt like a secret detective nosing into personal family problems where I wasn't invited.

But I did it because I was "called" to this position. When the bishop or branch president called us to a position, we didn't say no. He is *God's representative* on earth, we were told.

Jim advanced quickly from Sunday school teacher to superintendent of Sunday school, until he had a *call* to be the second counselor to the branch president. In this capacity, he had the same authority as the head of this small branch. The three of them worked as a team. But to me he confided, "It really makes me uncomfortable to be called *President Robertson*."

Soon I was called to the Primary presidency. I met with the Primary president and another lady to manage our part of the organized LDS program. I also taught cultural refinement lessons in Relief Society. I worked hard and faithfully studied for my teaching and organization assignments.

Because the small congregation of members was spread out all over northwest Arkansas, I served as taxi for several children whose parents couldn't bring them after school to Primary. So I drove an hour before and after our weekly meeting over rough rural roads, finishing up my already low supply of energy.

I felt more like a robot than a human being. Preparing

and carrying out Primary and Relief Society duties left me drained, with nothing left for my family. I forgot how to feel and how to express my emotions. I was supposed to depict joy in my life, to convey a positive image of Mormonism. But I found it hard to smile. It wasn't easy trying to earn my way to heaven as LDS doctrine taught. Even so, I wore the smiling mask of Mormonism in front of others.

THROUGH A FRIEND OF JIM'S, another building was rented to house the increasing numbers becoming a part of this small congregation. It was an old funeral home. I became more and more somber as we met weekly in the same room where funerals were conducted.

My Primary class met in the dark basement where the dead were embalmed. The dimly lit, morbid room housed an elevator that lifted bodies to a funeral chapel, casting a dark shadow over the *restored gospel* I was called to teach to these little ones.

I fed these Primary children a gospel, but not the good news of Jesus dying in our place to pay the debt of our sins, thus securing for us eternal life with Him in heaven. No, I taught them the LDS doctrine that we must earn, by works of righteousness, a place in one of three heavens.

"Heavenly Father and one of his wives gave birth to us in heaven," I taught. "They sent us to earth to gain a physical body. Our life here is a test to prove ourselves worthy to return to heaven. As Latter-day Saints, we must obey the commands given us through Heavenly Father's prophets. If we do, we may achieve the highest heaven—the Celestial Kingdom."

I hadn't read from Isaiah 64:6 that "all our righteous acts are like filthy rags" to God, because I had never studied God's Word, the Bible.

In trying to make myself righteous, and in teaching these little ones a false gospel, I planted rancid seeds. Those seeds would produce death in them and in my own children.

We met in the basement, where corpses were stored and infused with formaldehyde, replacing lifeblood. Meanwhile, the lifeblood in me was being replaced by the dead works of the laws and ordinances of Mormonism.

7

Friends in Zion

I PARKED OUTSIDE NELL'S HOUSE. It was 10:00 P.M. and it was cold out. Our Primary presidency meeting had lasted much longer than we'd hoped. Nell seemed reluctant to leave the car. "Judy, can I tell you something?" Her heavy breathing fogged the windshield.

"Sure, Nell."

"I don't have a single friend." Stunned, I couldn't think of a thing to say. This was the Primary president. The one who I thought always had it together. I'd been so impressed with her organized year's supply of food and smoothly run household, but had noticed she didn't smile much—an intense person. She ran her home and the Primary like a drill sergeant.

"Nell, what do you mean? You know everyone in the church."

"Yeah, I know everyone, but no one is my friend. I'd be afraid to tell anyone what really goes on in my mind."

"You can tell me, Nell. It won't go any further than this car."

"My life is miserable. It just doesn't seem worth all the work. Chuck, our oldest son, is in trouble with the law. I worry constantly that people will find out our family is having serious problems. And Mike is branch president. Everything's supposed to go smoothly if you obey the gospel. But it isn't. And I have no one to share this with."

I sat in shock, not knowing how to respond. Wasn't the branch president and his family supposed to be living an exemplary life? Nell couldn't have doubts, could she?

"Nell, let's talk again some other time. I'm cold, and Jim will wonder what's happened to me." We never got together again. Not too long after we'd talked, Nell, only forty-five years old, died of a heart attack. I grieved this loss, but most of all, I felt I'd let her down. I may have been the only one to whom she'd given a glimpse of the heavy load she carried. Life had become too burdensome for Nell, and she had no one to turn to. Hadn't Heavenly Father let her down, too?

I hadn't even thought to pray with Nell that night. My meaningless prayer life consisted of "Help me be a good Primary leader and to uphold Jim as he carries out his priesthood duties. Help us carry out the teachings of the church."

Nell tried harder than anyone I knew to keep all the laws and ordinances of the church. But she hadn't been able to have any more children after her second child, born fifteen years after the first one. It was the duty of the Mormon woman to bring down as many spirit babies as possible to give them bodies so they could return one day to Heavenly

Father—a flesh-and-bone god. We were all conceived by him and one of his wives in heaven. All the peoples of the earth are his *spirit children*. Nell tried to make up for not bringing more spirits to earth by working extra hard at other required duties of Mormonism. I worked hard, too. It seemed it was never enough, though.

Nell was buried in her all-white temple garment with her green fig-leaf apron tied around her waist—the one issued to all who are worthy enough to go through the temple. A vow Nell agreed to in the LDS temple states, "You do consecrate yourselves, your time, talents, and everything with which the Lord has blessed you or may bless you to the Church of Jesus Christ of Latter-day Saints; for the building up of the kingdom of God on the earth and the establishment of Zion." Nell had kept her vow.

The god of Mormonism has an insatiable appetite; conscientious people are his food.

————

I FELT CHALLENGED WEEKLY as I worked on completing my nursing degree, one class at a time, at the University of Arkansas. At least there I felt human, my mind expanded. After my microbiology class, I dropped by to see Elaine, a Mormon friend, who worked in the stacks of the campus library. "Judy, did you know there are volumes of anti-Mormon books down in the basement?" she said, her voice tense with concern.

"No, I didn't. I'd like to see them and check some out."

"Oh, Judy, didn't you know we're not supposed to read that kind of stuff? It's not faith promoting!"

"Oh? No, I didn't know. Well, forget it, then. I won't read any. I never knew there was literature written against the church."

"Boy, you really are naïve. We're supposed to be persecuted, you know. It's a sign that we're the true church."

There was a lot I didn't know, especially about the history of the church—so much to read. I had only read the stories about the early pioneers crossing the plains and the good character traits of the church prophets, things I'd taught to the Primary children.

This was the first I'd heard of anti-Mormon literature. The funny thing was, I was intensely curious about the books. But if the church authorities said we shouldn't read this kind of literature, then I wouldn't read it. They must have good reasons.

8

Temple Gods

J UST WAIT TILL YOU GO THROUGH the temple. It's glorious!" We heard this statement over and over from church
members.

My friend Elaine insisted, "It's the most spiritual experience I've ever had."

Finally, after one year of proving ourselves worthy, Jim
and I were eligible to be interviewed for a temple recommend. Interrogations by the branch president in Fayetteville
and a stake president in Mesa followed. We were approved.
We entered the Mesa LDS temple grounds in June 1967,
accompanied by our daughter, Janet, and son, Steve.

Unable to sleep for the excitement, I tossed most of the
night before. We rose early for this much-anticipated day.
Butterflies flipped in my stomach as questions popped into
my mind. *What goes on in there? What will we encounter to
gain this marvelous spiritual experience?*

As we parked our burgundy Pontiac at the side parking
lot, the huge white granite structure cast a long shadow in

the Arizona sunshine. We strolled under majestic palms, alongside fountains flanked by meticulous multicolored flowerbeds. The surroundings matched my expectations for a glorious spiritual experience.

We stepped into a huge hall, and temple workers dressed in white greeted us. Janet and Steve were taken by an older woman to an obscure room in the temple. We didn't know where they'd go or what would happen to them.

Jim and I were separated and taken to men's and women's dressing rooms. I felt strangely alone.

A female temple worker told me to remove my clothing as she handed me a white garment called a *shield*. I stood naked in a private cubicle and slipped the shield over my head. It looked like a sheet with a hole in it for my head, open on either side. Other women wearing shields sat on benches waiting their turn in the washing and anointing room. We didn't look at or speak to each other. We stared straight ahead with blank expressions on our faces.

At this point, I vaguely remember being told I would now be prepared, "cleansed from the blood and sins of this generation." The moments that followed are blocked from my memory. But after I listened to actual tape recordings of the temple ritual, I now know that a woman temple worker wets her hand in water and ceremonially washes every part of your body. She reaches under the shield lightly touching each body part as she recites words of the ceremony.

After the washing with water, I was led into another part of the room and seated on a thronelike chair. Another temple worker poured drops of oil from a large horn onto my head and into her own hand. Then she anointed each part of my body with oil to prepare me to become a "Queen and a priestess unto the Most High God, hereafter to rule and reign in the House of Israel forever."[1]

I didn't feel like a queen-in-waiting; I felt defiled, ashamed, and bewildered.

After the cleansing and anointing procedure, I received my special underwear.

"Sister Robertson, having authority, I place this garment upon you," the temple worker's arms reached under the shield, pulling the nylon one-piece undergarment on me. "It represents the garment given to Adam when he was found naked in the Garden of Eden, and is called the garment of the holy priesthood."

The garment covered me from neckline to cap sleeves and down, reaching to just above my knees. I felt uncomfortable and claustrophobic. "Inasmuch as you do not defile it, but are true and faithful to your covenants, it will be a shield and a protection to you against the power of the destroyer until you have finished your work on earth." I was told I must wear this garment of the holy priesthood next to my skin, even under ordinary underwear constantly, day and night, throughout my life.

"With this garment, I give you a new name, which you should always remember and which you must keep sacred, and never reveal except at a certain place that will be shown you hereafter." The temple worker whispered in my ear, "Your name is Augusta."

The washing and anointing procedure was supposed to cleanse me from the blood and sins of this generation. And yet I had been baptized eighteen years earlier in a Disciples

of Christ Christian church, in the name of Jesus for the re-
mission of sins.

How could I forget my treasure in Christ? I hadn't cher-
ished this wonderful gift. I had taken it for granted, and now
I was taking on something new. Like a lamb frozen in fear
before a roaring lion, I stood dumb, silent, and received a
new name—Augusta—instead of the name of Jesus. I had
been baptized into His name as a child. Now I sank into the
deep miry pit of oaths, tokens, and handshakes, and wore a
covering that shielded me from Jesus' love.

U SHERED BACK INTO THE DRESSING ROOM where I had
changed from my street clothes in the beginning and
into the white shield, I was now given the complete temple
frock—white slip, long white dress, white hose, and moc-
casins.

I joined other LDS women on their way to the endowment room. We padded silently down a huge hall and up a
winding stairway to a large theater. A temple worker ushered us into a row of comfortable seats.

Men sat on one side of the room, women on the other.
We were told to "maintain the quiet reverence that should
prevail in the House of the Lord." All of us sat there, looking
like so many sheep in our white temple clothing. I felt help-
less, as though something was being done to me that I had
no control over. I wanted to run and hide. But where would
I go?

Blood Oath

LARGE MURALS DEPICTING the Garden of Eden covered the walls of the Creation Room. We sat quietly, waiting to receive the first part of our *endowments*, whatever they were.

A man dressed in white introduced himself as the officiator. "Brethren and sisters, we welcome you to the temple, and hope you will find joy serving in the House of the Lord this day. . . . Please be alert, attentive, and refrain from whispering during the presentation of the endowment.

"Brethren . . . you have been anointed to become hereafter kings and priests unto the Most High God, to rule and reign in the House of Israel forever.

"Sisters, you have been washed and anointed to become queens and priestesses to your husbands."

The endowment ceremony would prepare us for exaltation in the Celestial Kingdom. The officiator said, "If you proceed and receive your full endowment, you will be required to take upon yourselves sacred obligations; the violation of which will bring upon you the judgment of God; for God will not be mocked. If any of you desires to withdraw rather than accept these obligations of your own free will and choice, you may now make it known by raising your hand." None of us raised our hand.

How do I know what sacred obligations I'll be taking? I cringed, and wondered, *Does anyone ever leave at this point? What would happen if I raised my hand?* I sat motionless and silent like all the other patrons.

I feel like running. . . . Why am I just sitting here? My mind said one thing, my body didn't move. *Just a little longer,* I sighed. *The spirituality part of the ceremony must be next.*

THREE MEN IN WHITE CLOTHES began a drama that depicted a strange version of Creation. A man represented *Elohim* and said to two others, "Jehovah, Michael, see. Yonder is matter unorganized. Go ye down and organize it into a world like unto the worlds that we have heretofore formed."

Matter unorganized? Organize it into a world? What are they talking about? I've never heard anything like this before. I squirmed in my seat, but made no effort to leave.

Several scenes later the narrator said, "Brethren and sisters, this is Michael, who helped form the earth. When he awakens from the sleep which Elohim and Jehovah have caused to come upon him, he will be known as Adam, and having forgotten all will become like a little child." The narrator instructed us, "Brethren, close your eyes as if you were asleep." We complied.

Did I literally go to sleep here? How could I ignore the blatant spiritual errors that were espoused? I'd been to church all my life. I knew God created the earth from nothing—not from matter that already existed. Who was this Michael who helped form the earth and then became Adam? Why didn't I get up and run out? *Why?*

The further the drama went, the more confusing it became. I looked around the room. Many heads bobbed. Several heads were unashamedly on their chests with eyes closed. *No wonder people are asleep—they can't figure out what's going on,* I thought.

The drama continued, depicting a perverted reenactment of the temptation of Adam and Eve in the Garden of Eden. Lucifer entered wearing a flowing crimson velvet robe with tunic and apron underneath it. Lucifer tempted Adam first. Adam refused to eat the fruit, whereupon Lucifer said, "Oh, you will not?" He looked at Eve with a wide grin and said, "Well, we shall see."

He walked to Eve, where she was admiring flowers. "Eve, here is some of the fruit of that tree." He held out some of the fruit to her. "It will make you wise. It is delicious to the taste and very desirable."

Eve said, "Who are you?"

Lucifer replied, "I am your brother."

"You, my brother, have come here to persuade me to disobey Father?"

"I have said nothing about Father," Lucifer said. "I want you to eat of the fruit of the Tree of Knowledge of Good and Evil, that your eyes may be opened, for that is the way Father gained his knowledge. You must eat of this fruit so as to comprehend that everything has its opposite—good and evil, virtue and vice, light and darkness, health and sickness, pleasure and pain—and thus your eyes will be opened and you will have . . . knowledge."

"Is there no other way?" Eve asked.

"There is no other way."

"Then I will partake."

Eve took a bite of the fruit.

Lucifer then told her, "There, now go and get Adam to partake."

Eve walked over to Adam and sweetly and persuasively said, "Adam, here is some of the fruit of that tree. It is delicious to the taste and very desirable."

Adam looked surprised. "Eve, do you know what fruit that is?"

"Yes," Eve said, "it is the fruit of the Tree of Knowledge of Good and Evil."

Adam said, "I cannot partake of it. Do you know that Father commanded us not to partake of the fruit of that tree?"

"Do you intend to obey all of Father's commandments?"

"Yes, all of them."

"Do you not recollect that Father commanded us to multiply and replenish the earth? I have partaken of this fruit and, by so doing, shall be cast out. And you will be left a lone man in the Garden of Eden."

"Eve, I see that this must be so. I will partake that man may be."

Lucifer came on the scene. "That is right."

Eve said, "It is better for us to pass through sorrow that we may know the good from the evil." Eve turned to Lucifer. "I know thee now. Thou art Lucifer, he who was cast out of Father's presence for rebellion."

"Yes, you are beginning to see already."

Adam asked, "What is that apron you have on?"

Lucifer answered, "It is an emblem of my power and priesthoods."

"Priesthoods?"

"Yes, priesthoods," Lucifer responded.

"I am looking for Father to come down to give us further instructions."

"Oh, you are looking for Father to come down, are you?"

Elohim's voice is heard from a distance. "Jehovah, we promised Adam that we would visit him and give him further instructions. Come, let us go down."

Jehovah said, "We will go down, Elohim."

Adam said, "I hear voices; they are coming."

Lucifer warned them, "See, you are naked. Take some fig leaves and make you aprons. Father will see your nakedness. Quick! Hide!"

Adam became alarmed and said, "Come, let us hide."

The narrator interrupted the drama and instructed us, "Brethren and sisters, put on your aprons." We tied bright green satin aprons embroidered with fig leaves around our waists. Throughout the temple ceremony, we never removed the green fig-leaf apron Lucifer instructed us to put on.

THE DRAMA CONTINUED as Adam and Eve were cast out of the Garden. Then discussion followed in which Lucifer threatened Elohim and defiantly said, "If thou curseth me for doing the same thing which has been done in other worlds, I will take the spirits that follow me, and they shall possess the bodies thou createst for Adam and Eve."

Elohim replied, "I will place enmity between thee and the seed of the woman. Thou mayest have power to bruise his heel, but he shall have power to crush thy head."

Lucifer threatened again, "Then, with that enmity, I will take the treasures of the earth; and with gold and silver I will buy up armies and navies, popes and priests, and reign with blood and horror on this earth."

I wish I could remember some of the statements about Satan's power in the Bible. He seems scary in this drama. Elohim cowered before him. My mind seemed non-functional, unable to make sense of the strange drama I watched as though chained to my seat.

After telling Lucifer to depart, Elohim said, "We will put the sisters under covenant to obey the laws of their husbands. Sisters, arise." We stood obediently.

"Each of you bring your right arm to the square." All of us women brought our arms up at right angles. "You and each of you solemnly covenant and promise before God, angels, and these witnesses at this altar that you will each observe and keep the law of your husband and abide by his counsel in righteousness. Each of you bow your head and say yes."

"Yes," our voices sounded in unison.

Will Jim always tell me righteous things? What about

obedience to God? It seemed the ceremony would never end.

Elohim said, "That will do." And all of us women sat down.

Elohim said to the men, "Brethren, arise. Bring your right arm to the square." The men then raised their arms to right angles. "You and each of you solemnly covenant and promise before God, angels, and these witnesses at this altar that you will obey the law of God and keep His command-ments. Each of you bow your head and say yes." The men did as they were told. Bowing their heads, their voices mum-bled a monotone "Yes."

Elohim said, "That will do." Their temple garments swished as they sat down.

My mind hazily focused on the covenant I'd just made. All my life I had tried to please others. Never had I openly rebelled against anyone who had been in authority over me, but neither had I ever had an authority figure tell me any-thing that seemed strange before.

Will this never end? I felt hot and uncomfortable. But it was far from over.

The *tokens* of the Aaronic and Melchizedek priesthoods, their accompanying name, sign, and penalties, would drag on, and with them, more of my own will to resist. I agreed to accept each as they explained them, even agreeing to have my life taken by the cutting of my throat if I revealed any of it.

The officiator showed us what to do. "Each of you make the sign of the first token of the Aaronic priesthood by bringing your right arm to the square, the palm of the hand to the front, the fingers close together, and the thumb extended. Now, repeat in your minds after me the words of the covenant, at the same time representing the execution of the penalty."

I joined the rest and said, "I, Augusta (the new name whispered in my ear earlier), covenant that I will never reveal the first token of the Aaronic priesthood, with its accompanying name, sign, and penalty. Rather than do so, I would suffer," all of us placed our thumbs under our left ear, palms down, "my life," we drew our thumbs across our throats quickly to the right ear, "to be taken." We all dropped our right hands down to our sides.

"That will do," the officiator said, and we all sat down.[1]

Gateway to Hell

A WITNESS COUPLE WAS CALLED FORWARD and knelt at an altar. The officiator demonstrated the procedure for the second token of the Aaronic priesthood, using this couple as models. We were to copy their actions, and were instructed to use our own first given name in taking the covenant if we were going through the temple for the first time. If this were not our first time, we were going through for the dead and would use the dead person's name.

I felt nauseous. Most of the people around me were using the names of dead people. Again I felt like running, but it was like the nightmare I had so many times as a child, where I was running from some horrible thing that was chasing me—but I ran in slow motion, the thing right on my heels. My mouth moved in those dreams in a scream, but no sounds would come out. I would awaken making guttural sounds in my throat, my heart beating wildly. This, too, had to be a bad dream. But somehow I could not escape from this nightmare. It was real.

The name, signs, and penalties of the second token of the Aaronic priesthood, the first and second tokens of the Melchizedek priesthood, the Law of Chastity, and the Law of Consecration followed. We performed, like robots, the grotesque actions of having our chest ripped open and our bowels slashed if we revealed any of it. *What had happened to my mind? Why did I not resist any of this?*

We stood to enact the "sure sign of the nail." Following the officiator's example, we raised our arms high above our heads and chanted, *"Pay lay ale,"* lowering our arms, palms down, slowly. We raised and lowered our arms three times chanting these words. I felt completely foolish.

The officiator told us, "When Adam was driven out of the Garden of Eden, he built an altar and offered prayer, and these are the words he used [*pay lay ale*], which interpreted are, 'O God, hear the words of my mouth.' "[1]

When we were in the Creation Room, it was Lucifer who answered this prayer. Why are we repeating the same words now? I thought.

We were told we would next hear a lecture. *How can I possibly go any further?* Time had blurred in my mind. Several hours already had gone by.

THE PURPOSE OF THIS LECTURE is to assist you to remember that which has been taught to you this day. You must keep in mind that you are under a solemn obligation never to speak, outside of these walls, of the things you see and hear in this sacred place."

Why must we keep all this a secret? I shivered. *If I ever get out of this building, I will be too ashamed to tell anyone what I have participated in.* I felt humiliated, like a child. And like a child I wanted to crawl under the chairs and sneak out. But I stayed like all the rest.

We were ushered into another room, where we were instructed to form a circle. For the first time since our separation at the men's and women's lockers, I saw Jim. *He looks so strange wearing that baker-type hat, as all the men do. We all look pretty stupid,* I thought as I gazed around the circle. *It's hard to be serious when we look like circus clowns.* I fought back a laugh while, at the same time, I chastised myself for feeling this way.

As we stood in the circle, the officiator gave instructions. He taught meanings of secret signs and handshakes we needed to know and oaths to repeat when we got to the veil where we would repeat them to the "Lord." I was tired and found it hard to concentrate. It had been at least three hours of instruction, and we weren't finished.

On and on, the ceremony drew me deeper and deeper into its occultic ritual. Then came the pinnacle of the ceremony at the veil. It was an enormous white sheet with symbols on it like the ones on the garments of the holy priesthood I wore, except on my garments the symbols were in miniature. I stood staring at this veil. I wore a billowy white dress over the temple garment. I thought momentarily, *Only the men can hold the priesthood. Then why do I, a woman, wear the garment, too?*

The man behind the veil said he was the "Lord," and I must repeat to him all the names, signs, and tokens I had learned from the endowment ceremony.

The officiator explained each shape. One puzzled me. "This is the knee mark," he said. "It's placed on the right leg of the garment over the knee, and indicates that every knee shall bow and every tongue confess that Jesus is the Christ."

It doesn't sound right, I thought. *The demons knew He was the Christ, too, didn't they?* I wished I'd known my Bible better. *Isn't it, "Every knee shall bow and every tongue confess that Jesus Christ is Lord"?* So many things I heard sounded familiar and yet not quite right. Then I thought of a phrase Jim said so often, "Close only counts in horseshoes."

But what does it matter? Doesn't it mean the same?

———

M Y IDEA OF A VEIL is a soft, billowy, see-through material—like something a bride wears over her face. This veil looked more like a plain white bed sheet to me, except for the shapes cut in it.

As I stood next to the veil, a temple worker, called an "introducer," stood next to me. She tapped three times on something wooden with a small mallet. The man who called himself the "Lord" parted the veil from the other side and peeked out slightly, saying, "What is wanted?"

The temple worker explained that I desired further light and knowledge by conversing with the "Lord" through the veil.

"Present her at the veil and her request shall be granted," he said.

As I stood silently wondering what would happen next, the temple worker positioned me in front of the "Lord." The

"Lord" thrust his right hand through one of the slashes in the veil and took my right hand. I cooperated with the various hand grips and replied to the "Lord's" questions, prompted by the temple worker as to what each name and sign represented.

As the ritual continued, the temple worker said I had not yet received the following *name*, and the "Lord" replied, "You shall receive it [simultaneously] upon the five points of fellowship through the veil."

The "Lord" then embraced me in these five points. The inside of his right foot was placed inside my right foot, his knee to mine, his breast to mine, his hand to my back, his mouth to my ear, all the while still holding my hand in the Patriarchal Grip. I could feel the warmth of this unknown man's body next to mine. Although the veil was between us, his hot breath was in my ear. I felt I would faint. My face flushed.

The temple worker told me to repeat after her. "Health in the navel; marrow in the bones; strength in the loins and in the sinews; power in the priesthood be upon me and upon my posterity through all generations of time and throughout all eternity." After this incantation, the "Lord" released me from his embrace and withdrew his arms. I breathed a sigh of relief, but felt defiled, molested. Only my husband ever held me that close.

The "Lord" then asked, "What is wanted?"

The temple worker said, "Judy, having conversed with the 'Lord' through the veil, desires to enter his presence."

The "Lord" then took my arm and pulled me through to the other side of the veil and said solemnly, "Let her enter." The elegantly furnished room I entered, called the Celestial Room, represented the highest degree of glory. I waited quietly on a blue French Provincial chair for Jim to come through the veil. We would join each other and have our marriage sealed for time and all eternity.

As Jim came through the veil, I looked anxiously at him, hoping to talk. But that was squelched when a temple worker approached and quickly ushered us to a sealing room. An altar draped with purple velvet cloth dominated the room with great mirrors on either side that gave the appearance of looking into infinity. We were told to stand together at the center of the room while instructions were given and then to kneel at the altar. Kneeling there, I remember hearing, "Look at each other and then into the mirrors. You can see forever. That's how your marriage will be—sealed for eternity."

Janet and Steve were brought in by an older woman. They, too, were dressed in white clothes. The temple worker brought them to us, and they knelt beside us. They'd apparently been instructed what to do. They were included in the remainder of the sealing ceremony, which was to bind us together for eternity. They were dazed—so was I.

After the agonizing five-hour ceremony ended, Larry stood with tears in his eyes. He had joined us for this important event. We'd taken the missionary lessons in his home. I couldn't understand why he was crying. I felt uncomfortable and wanted out as soon as possible.

On the steps outside the temple, Jim asked, "What kind of 'Mickey Mouse' ceremony was that?"

"I don't know, Jim. It seems meaningless and weird." We

searched for answers in each other's eyes. "It definitely was not the glorious spiritual experience we'd been told we would have."

Later we shared with Larry and Lyn, "The ceremony seemed strange to us—we're not comfortable with it."

"You'll get the full significance once you've been through it several times," Lyn said with a nervous laugh. "From now on you will go through the ceremony for someone who is dead."

Several times? I would have to go through this again? I shuddered. *And for dead people? Oh no.*

Jim and I didn't talk to each other about the temple ceremony after we told Lyn and Larry our feelings. After all, we'd taken oaths not to reveal even to each other the secret, or "sacred," temple rituals we'd just been through.

We traveled back to Fayetteville with something new in our lives. We were now *temple Mormons* and wore the garments of the holy priesthood. I felt as though an enormous collar was around my physical body.

I literally partook of the lie of Satan, as did my husband, Jim, that day. It would change the course of my life as I took a bite of that forbidden fruit just as Eve did . . . in the beginning.

11

Redundant Life

JIM, THIS LOOKS SO GROTESQUE!" I struggled to pull my
panties up over my temple garment. Now as temple Mormons we had a new responsibility. We were to wear the full-
length garment next to our skin at all times. We were told
in the temple, "It will be a shield and a protection to you if
you are true and faithful to your covenants."

"The garment just won't go on smoothly. It's all rumpled and lopsided," I said, stretching and pulling at the full-
length jumpsuit. "And look! My bra won't even stay in place
on top of this slippery nylon!" Tears ran down my cheeks.
"Now it looks like I don't have any breasts at all!"

Jim drew me close and wiped my tears. "I'm having a
hard time, too. I feel like I have on long-handle underwear
all the time."

I longed for someone to talk to, but I didn't dare tell my
Mormon sisters about the darkness I felt inside. I had just
been to the temple. I was supposed to come back ecstatic
and with renewed vigor for my Mormon duties.

I charged into my activities as though nothing was wrong. But it became increasingly difficult to function. Passing by a mirror one morning, I caught a glimpse of myself. My shoulders slumped; my face showed a furrowed brow and pursed lips. I tried straightening my blouse and knee-length shorts, but it didn't help. Even though no one could see the garments, I thought I looked disheveled, like I had ill-fitting clothes on. I didn't like the feel of the garment under my clothes.

We weren't the only LDS members having problems with the garments. One of my friends who taught in Primary came to Jim for marriage counseling. "Just once I'd like to feel my husband's body next to mine without the garment on. But he refuses to remove it even during our most intimate times." Their marriage ended in divorce.

Thank goodness we didn't go that far. But I had gotten rid of the feminine nighties in my drawer. They would look funny on top of the garment.

Most of the sisters wore dowdy dresses that looked similar to what a pioneer woman would wear in an attempt to cover it. Dresses and tops required sleeves to fit over the garment's cap sleeves. Clothing length was a problem, too, and most shorts were out. Only mid-knee ones would cover the garment that stopped just above the knee. It was a constant struggle to keep it from peeking out from beneath my clothes.

I felt dehumanized and old. Jim worked long hours at his job, and I felt alone in my struggle. Life didn't seem worth living anymore.

W ELL, HI, JUDY," Dr. Patrick, our family doctor, said cheerfully. I sat frozen, unable to respond. "What's wrong? Are you pregnant?" A lump swelled in my throat. "Are you and Jim having problems?" My tears began to roll. I could no longer hold back the turbulence built up inside, and I sobbed hysterically.

"Wait here. We'll draw some blood, and then I want you to go home and get some rest." A nurse came in to draw a vial of blood and give me a shot.

"Do you have anyone to drive you home?" I didn't. But the shot worked so fast they had to call Jim to drive me home. I slept for hours.

Dr. Patrick called a few days later. "Your blood work looks good, Judy. Your hemoglobin is down a bit, so I want you to take some iron tablets that I'll call in for you." And then without hesitating he added, "I'd like you to see a psychiatrist." He gave me the number of a doctor he recommended. "Don't delay. Call and make an appointment today."

I trusted Dr. Patrick, although the thought of a psychiatrist filled me with dread and fear. What would he ask and what could I tell him? I couldn't tell about the temple ceremony and what we'd gone through. I'd taken a blood oath not to reveal any of it. I had drawn my thumb across my neck and my lower abdomen saying I'd submit to having "my throat cut and my bowels ripped out" if I ever did. The thought made my blood run cold.

How could I possibly justify counseling? It was expensive. My stomach tied in knots and I didn't know what I could possibly tell him that would help me. Only my misery propelled me into the office of this strange doctor.

I stiffened as my name was called and moved toward his office in a daze. After some small talk, he asked questions about my family. I openly told of my sister's problems. I freely expounded on hers and conveniently avoided my own. I felt angry and judgmental.

"Who do you think you are—God?" the stony doctor asked.

I froze in my chair, unable to respond. He'd driven words, like swords, right into my gut. Who did I think I was, anyway? The audacity of me, to judge my sister when my life was falling to pieces—from the garment out.

I terminated these visits before I had to reveal anything else. I was humiliated and scared. I hadn't been able to talk to anyone. I had no friends—suddenly it hit me—that's just what Nell had said, *"I have no friends, Judy."*

I'd seen the garment rumpled under Nell's otherwise neat clothing, topped off with her stern-but-determined look. But the most chilling picture in my mind was how she looked in the casket. At the time, I was puzzled by the white temple clothes on her lifeless body, with the green apron around her waist. But since I'd now participated in the temple ceremony, I understood why she was dressed that way.

One of the drama scenes in the temple ceremony depicts Lucifer instructing Adam and Eve to make fig-leaf aprons to cover their nakedness. We were provided aprons, and we wore them for the remainder of the temple rituals. Even in Nell's death she wore the covering of Lucifer. *But hadn't God given Adam and Eve animal skins to wear?* I put this question aside to consider at a later time. There had to be some deep meaning I hadn't yet grasped.

I took on more and more of Nell's characteristics. I performed my Mormon duties robot-like, putting on a smile mask when necessary, removing it behind closed doors. *I must endure to the end,* I reasoned. *But I hope the end is near.*

Jim helped the growing branch secure property—the elders considered it divine providence—on Zion Road. A fine brick ward building soon stood on a hill overlooking prime northwest Arkansas property.

Standard blueprints came from the church office in Salt Lake City, as well as 90 percent of the needed funds to build the church. The remaining 10 percent of the costs were assessed from the sweat-earned dollars of the saints by the branch presidency. No one even considered *not* paying what the priesthood leaders assessed them. Each family must do their share to advance the church's work. After all, "When the prophet speaks, the thinking has been done. There is no need to think on it," President George Smith had said. He was president five years before David O. McKay, the prophet in office when we joined the church.

The priesthood leaders in our branch followed the line of authority from the prophet, having had hands laid on them to receive the Melchizedek priesthood. And the people obeyed them as they would the voice of God.

I often wondered why those who lived in the backwoods had to contribute, too. They drove old beat-up cars that barely ran. Their children's clothes were often torn and dirty. They could have used a pair of shoes, too.

It seemed those who were the poorest had the most children. But they were proud to bring all the spirit babies down from heaven to give them physical bodies. These children could now live on earth, prepare to be like Heavenly Father, and progress to the Celestial Kingdom.

Where was the God I had learned about as a child? He seemed so far away.

12

Westward, Ho!

JOE AND LARRY TRAVELED from Arizona to talk with Jim about their business—potatoes. "We want you to go into business with us, Jim." They talked about plans to put a potato chip factory in Queen Creek close to the potato fields. "What do you think? You'll be near the temple and your family will benefit from the expanded programs of the church," Joe added.

The offer was enticing. Even though it meant selling our businesses, leaving both sides of our family, a home we had designed ourselves, and the university town we'd lived in for twelve years. The benefit of being among other Mormons was the big draw.

I dreaded this move, knowing it would happen no matter how I felt. "We won't be near your folks or mine anymore, Jim." I hoped he'd reconsider. After all, our family had blossomed to three children when I delivered our delightful son, Kirk. "Our kids will miss their grandparents and cousins."

But Jim was the priesthood holder in our family, and the decision was final. I didn't like it, but I didn't argue.

The women and children were to place the priesthood members on a pedestal. After all, I had seen the line of authority from which Jim received his priesthood. Joseph Smith had received the priesthood from Peter, James, and John, and they received theirs from Jesus Christ. It had been passed on to Jim in this direct line. Who was I to argue with that? It was taught regularly in Relief Society and in Primary.

Living in Arkansas, we weren't able to make regular trips to a temple. The closest one was in Arizona, 1,300 miles away. LDS members sometimes used their life savings to pilgrimage to one of the forty-seven Mormon temples throughout the world. We hadn't been back through the temple since our first visit. Maybe we'd view it in a different light now.

I left thoughts of the temple ceremonies tucked neatly away somewhere in my subconscious. We had taken vows in the temple never to speak of it again. We had told our Mormon friends, Larry and Lyn, how bizarre we thought the proceedings were after the ceremony that sealed our marriage for time and all eternity. But there the discussion ended, on the top step as we left the temple, never to be picked up again.

But things stuffed in the subconscious have a way of leaking out anyway, no matter how far down they're pushed. Depression haunted me for seven years. *Something must be wrong with me,* I thought. *Everyone else in the Mormon Church seems okay. All these good, upstanding, kind people— they all seem happy. What is wrong with me?*

It would be easier to live the Mormon lifestyle in Mesa, surrounded by so many church members. Our kids would belong to a close-knit group of Latter-day Saints. We could buy our year's supply of food without seeming strange. No one would think twice if the garment peeked from under my skirt. We'd still suffer persecution, but the church taught that this only proves we are the only true church on earth today.

ONE EVENING, shortly before we left for Arizona, John Maguire and his son, Dale, came to call. John and his wife, Lorene, were longtime friends before we became Mormons. John had recently accepted Christ.

"Jim and Judy, you know my family and I love you two dearly," John began. "I just want to know, how's your relationship with Christ?"

"It's fine, John," Jim assured him. "We have a good relationship with Christ, we simply have more now—more scriptures. We follow the Bible where it lays out the foundation of the church. I'll read it from our *Articles of Faith*, number six, 'We believe in the same organization that existed in the Primitive Church, namely, apostles, prophets, pastors, teachers, evangelists, and so forth.' Number eight says, 'We believe the Bible to be the word of God as far as it is translated correctly; we also believe the *Book of Mormon* to be the word of God.' " Jim obediently recited the doctrine taught to him.

"It sounds okay, Jim," John nodded, "but I don't know anything about the Mormon religion." John stood a foot above Jim and me. His words had a pleading tone, "I'm just concerned about your relationship with Christ. Dale and I came over because we wanted to be sure you two were right with the Lord. I don't want you to take off for Arizona without a chance to talk to you first."

"Be assured, everything's fine, John. Couldn't be better."

"Before we leave, Jim and Judy, do you mind if we pray? Praying is pretty new to me, but I'd like to give it a try, okay?"

"Great, John. We'd love to pray."

John, Dale, Jim, and I held hands in our living room and bowed our heads. John prayed for us all. We shook hands as they walked out the front door. But when the door shut behind them, Jim shook his head, "Isn't it a shame the Maguires don't have all the truth as we do?"

"Yes, it is, Jim." I nodded my head. "Such good people, too."

A RIZONA NEVER SEEMED SO HOT as the first day of June 1972. Jim drove the heavily loaded U-Haul with all our earthly belongings. I drove our blue Oldsmobile Cutlass Supreme with Janet, Steve, and Kirk in the backseat.

Joe let us park the U-Haul on the back lot of the potato shed in Queen Creek while we drove into Mesa to find a motel. We went to the area we were familiar with, close to the temple and Pioneer Park.

The El Rancho Motel had a little kitchenette and a swimming pool. "This will do us temporarily, hon. Shouldn't take too long to find a place to live," Jim assured us. We cooled off our hot, tired bodies in the swimming pool and went to bed early.

We drove to East Mesa the next morning to find a home. I needed to fill the empty spot created when we pulled up our roots in Arkansas. We had left extended family, a beautiful home on a wooded lot, friends of twelve years, and Jim's businesses. We left it all to make ourselves better Mormons, to attend the temple, to do works for the dead, and work our way to heaven.

––––––––––

WE SETTLED COMFORTABLY in a four-bedroom home on the edge of town, next to corn and cotton fields. "The kids will have lots of room to run and play. Steve is going to miss the woods, though, Jim. Kirk, too," I worried aloud. "I sure hope Janet finds a friend soon."

"Mom, I don't think Suzy will like this fence in our backyard. Beagles like to hunt, and she's used to running free." Janet came in from a romp with our family pet we'd brought from Arkansas. "But look at Kirk. He's buzzing through that dusty field with his Big Wheel."

"It's so barren. I hope we can get grass in soon, Jim," I lamented.

"We will. We will. One thing at a time. I've got to get the potato chip deal going first."

But the factory never materialized. After visiting grocery stores, inspecting property and equipment, Jim's research revealed the dream was not realistic. What started out to be one price to get the business going ended up being three times that amount.

"I've been this route before," Jim mused, "and I'm just not going to get caught up in heavy debt again." He thumped his pencil loudly on the kitchen table. "I'll have to find something else."

While transferring funds from the sale of our businesses and home in Arkansas to a bank in Mesa, Jim made friends with the manager. "We need someone like you to organize our personnel department, Jim. Why don't you put in your application in the main office in Phoenix?"

Personnel business was Jim's forte. He had owned and run a personnel agency in Fayetteville and Tulsa, Oklahoma. "Why not?" And after a series of interviews, Jim was hired in August 1972 at the largest financial institution in Arizona.

"We came out here to build a potato chip factory and go to the temple!" I wailed. "And you said the kids could get a horse! Now you've taken a job in Phoenix? How are we going to enjoy the activities of the ward here in Mesa when you have to travel twenty miles a day to Phoenix?" I had become a down-the-line Mormon, doing whatever I must to walk the straight and narrow. But I was still grieving from our move from Fayetteville. Jim took the brunt of the loneliness I felt. After my outburst, I felt guilty because I wasn't upholding the "priesthood."

We began attending the Mormon chapel near our home, the thirty-third ward, on Brown Road. The Primary president was away for the summer. "Sister Robertson, I want you to take the president's position for the summer," Bishop Nelson said.

"All right, Bishop, I will." In addition, I agreed to be a Cub Scout den mother in our ward. And so I charged right back into the work of the church practically before our new flooring was installed.

Part Three

Light to Blinded Eyes

13

Light Dawns

As Cub Scout den mother, it was my turn to host the meeting. "I saw Brother Mack smoking. He's really bad." Two little Cub Scouts sat on our back patio with their navy blue shirts and caps and bright yellow kerchiefs around their necks.

"Yeah, he's breaking the Word of Wisdom. He won't be able to go to the temple, my mom said."

"Boys, drinking coffee and smoking are bad habits, but it doesn't mean the person is bad," I insisted.

"But you can't go to the temple if you do, Sister Robertson."

"You're right," I went on. "The prophet taught we should stay away from tobacco and drinking alcohol, coffee, and tea. Keeping the Word of Wisdom is a requirement to go inside the temple, the 'House of the Lord.'"

"Well, if smoking and drinking coffee and stuff don't make you bad, then why can't you go in?"

"It's the law of the temple, Jeremy."

I couldn't think of a good answer for these little guys. In fact, the question hung around in the recesses of my mind, popping up occasionally. *Why can't so-called good people go into the temple?* I wondered. *And only a choice few remain temple worthy after they've been in the first time.* Maybe I was also unworthy because of the questions that kept coming into my mind. They certainly weren't faith promoting.

Like cancer, my guilt spread. I didn't have a year's supply of food and essentials stored in our home. Every time my friend, who had a bountiful food storage in her home, reminded me, "You'd better get with the program," I felt my chest tighten.

How in the world will I be able to gather all this together when we are functioning on such a tight budget right now?

I bought two 50-pound containers of whole-wheat berries and a 100-pound sack of pinto beans. At least I had some essentials. I supposed our family wouldn't starve if there was a national emergency, a natural disaster, or if Jim lost his job. The church recommended it so we'd be prepared.

I wanted to do what was right, but it seemed I could never measure up to the standards. The load of guilt was unbearable. I never felt relieved of my sense of failure to live up to every requirement. It was like an albatross around my neck.

A CLASS ON GENEALOGY and family exaltation was offered during Sunday school. I took the class knowing I desperately needed to work on our family's genealogy, but I didn't have the time to do it.

We wouldn't be able to do any of our ancestors' work in the temple if I didn't get this done. "Our dead relatives are waiting for us to be baptized in proxy for them in the temple," we were taught. An accurate record was essential. But none of my family had ever kept their history, so this was going to be a monumental task.

Knowing this work had to be done, I needed a goad to press me on. Already feeling the stress of my church jobs, I couldn't see how I would possibly find time for one more obligation.

I'm doing everything I possibly can to live the "gospel." Why do I always feel guilty? I began to dread going to church on Sundays.

Surely I could find scriptures that would spur me on to tackle this responsibility with zeal, I thought.

After class on Sunday, I brought out my King James Bible published by the Mormon press, Deseret Book Company in Salt Lake City, Utah. It had a beautiful picture of the Sea of Galilee on the front cover and Jerusalem's ancient wall on the back. Nothing was unusual about it except that it had an extensive concordance, index, and other special helps in the back.

I laid the Bible on the kitchen table along with a yellow legal pad and pencil, turned to the concordance, and looked up *genealogy*. It was not listed there. I looked in the index. There it was, at the end of a list of Old Testament references to genealogy and the genealogy of Christ in Matthew and

Luke. "Endless," it said, and listed only 1 Timothy 1:4. It ended with "See Fables."

I quickly turned to the passage in Timothy. "Neither give heed to fables and endless genealogies, which minister questions, rather than godly edifying which is in faith." Stunned, I wondered, *What does this mean? Don't do genealogies? But that's one of the essential works of the church.*

There was a cross-reference down the middle of the page, but none that had to do with genealogy. "God, I don't understand. Your Word says to avoid genealogies, and yet the church teaches it's the most important work we do. I'm confused. We joined the Mormon Church thinking this was your will. We alienated family and friends and moved to Arizona to be near your temple. Please tell me what this means." I left this prayer with God and didn't tell another soul about my questions.

SOMETIMES WHEN I COULDN'T FALL ASLEEP at night I picked up the *Reader's Digest* and hazily read a light article. It usually helped steer my thoughts away from the heavy burdens I carried. It had been about three weeks since I presented my special request to God.

I read a story about childhood and freedom before I fell asleep this particular night. I awakened an hour or so after midnight feeling depressed. Thinking of my own children and the burden they, too, would carry as Mormons weighed me down.

I got up and wandered about the dark house. There in the quietness of the early morning hour, oblivious to the passage of time, I knelt on the carpet in the living room. Quiet before God, no words came to my mind to pray. But during this act of humility, He reached into the very depths of my being.

A thought came to me. *Wouldn't Jesus allow someone into His house who smokes or drinks coffee?* The question seemed suspended and frozen in my mind. And then came the answer as clear and pure as a beam of light: *Of course Jesus would allow those who drink coffee or smoke into His house. Jesus invites the sinner in.*

Other thoughts flew into my mind one after another: *Would Jesus do this? Would He do that?* All the questions were related to LDS doctrine. It was as though pieces of a puzzle were dumped out of a bucket and pulled together like magnets, each into its own place.

The picture materialized. *The teachings of the church are not the teachings of Jesus. They are the teachings of man.*

Suddenly a blanket of peace surrounded me. *The LDS Church is not true. Jesus' words alone are true.* Jesus—that's what I'd been missing all along.

I felt as though a great load had been lifted from my shoulders. *Jesus is all I need. Jesus alone. Nothing else.*

Joy filled me. I was lifted up and set free. The exhilaration of the moment overwhelmed me. I sat on the living room floor soaking up the dawn—the light I had been given. Jesus entered my life profoundly, and surely would never leave me. Truth permeated my being, and I knew I no longer needed man's frail ways.

14

Set Free

WHAT ARE YOU DOING UP so early?" Jim mumbled as he observed my obvious been-up-for-a-while look. A surge of adrenaline hit the pit of my stomach. *How am I going to tell him what happened last night?*

Our communication with each other was at an all-time low. Not only because of my constant stress of striving to live up to Mormon standards, but because Jim had resigned from teaching his Sunday school class and had lost interest in attending church altogether. He went only to keep peace in the family. But there was no peace. Just tension and bottled-up feelings.

There was a foreboding silence hovering over our marriage. We were at odds with each other, and the strain of living in this atmosphere threatened to tear our bond apart at the seams.

But the events of the night were life changing. I wouldn't be able to keep it inside long. Excitement and fear created a potential explosion of words waiting to burst forth, but I had to contain it until the right time. "Jim, I've got something very important to tell you. But it will have to wait until tonight. There's just not enough time right now. And this is going to take a while."

Jim stared at me over the rim of a large glass of orange juice and then got ready for his commute to Phoenix.

Already out on the front sidewalk, the whirring of four-year-old Kirk's Big Wheel made the day seem regular. "Mom, can Ryan come over? And Matt, too?" The three were a team and had been since the summer before, when we moved into our new house. Ryan's family was Mormon and lived directly behind our house. He and Kirk went to Primary together. Ryan's mother, Donna, and I taught Primary together.

How will I tell Donna? She's such a dear friend . . . And the rest of my friends in the ward? I worried throughout the day. I dreaded this. But the most important thing was to tell Jim what had happened during the night.

On the one hand, I felt free as a bird, and yet there were butterflies turning somersaults in my stomach as though I were on the brink of a precipice getting ready to jump off.

Janet slept late. She had stayed overnight with a girl-friend. Steve, busy drawing a cartoon, helped me keep a sense of balance. *This isn't the end of the world. I will be able to get through this,* I tried to convince myself.

THE DAY THAT SEEMED LIKE A WEEK finally ended. With supper over, the kids cleared the dishes. One by one, I tucked them in for the night. The house was now quiet; the time had come for the telling. Tension filled every muscle.

I walked slowly into our family room where Jim sat, hands resting behind his head and leaning back against the couch. He looked up at the ceiling. "Okay, let's get on with this. What is it you have to tell me?"

I knew I'd have to be bold. No turning back now. This was it. It had to be quick. It had to be decisive. Like diving off the high-dive board for the first time—afraid and yet wanting to do it.

My stomach tied in knots, I sat down facing my husband and said slowly, "Jim, the Mormon Church is not true!" His mouth dropped open, and his hands came from behind his head with eyes widened.

"What?!" he said so loudly I thought the neighbors could hear. "Where in the world did you come up with an idea like that?"

"Do you remember three weeks ago when I did a word search on genealogy?"

"Yes, vaguely."

"Well, I found some verses in the Bible that disturbed me in 1 Timothy 1:4 and Titus 3:9. They seemed to say to avoid genealogies. It really got to me, Jim. I couldn't figure out why, if the church puts so much emphasis on genealogies, the Bible says to avoid it.

"So I prayed to God and asked Him to show me the meaning of it. Then, early this morning, I woke up really depressed and crying. I went into the living room, got down on my knees, and God opened my eyes, Jim. We've been following a false religion." I finished the story in detail, telling him all that had happened that morning.

Jim seemed entranced with what I said. "You know, Judy, what you're saying is like a tape recording going off in my head." Now it was my turn to be amazed. "When you first told me your discovery, my gut feeling was to defend the church. It just came automatically. But some of the things you're saying are exactly what I've been going through."

"You mean you've been having questions, too?"

"Yes," Jim sighed.

"But why didn't you tell me?"

"I was afraid to. You've always been so obedient to everything the leaders of the church said. I figured you wouldn't understand. And all day long, today, I thought you were going to ask me for a divorce or maybe tell me you were pregnant. I didn't know what to expect. I've been uptight all day."

"That makes two of us." I laughed with relief. "I worried all day about how to tell you this. It's hard for me to believe you've had questions, too."

"About a year ago, I decided that since I've never read through the Bible, I'd try to do it," Jim related. "The part in Genesis, chapter 3, about the serpent tempting Adam and Eve, and saying, 'You will be like God,' really caused me to think about what we are trying to achieve as Mormon men—to be gods of our own planets. But I dismissed that thought from my mind quickly. I kept reading on until I got to Isaiah 14," he continued. "Now that took me by surprise. It talks about Lucifer trying to exalt himself above the throne of God."

Jim talked fast, wanting to tell me the whole series of

events. "On the way home from work one day, this thought was heavy on my mind about becoming a god. I picked up the *Ensign* magazine, or maybe it was the *Improvement Era*—one of the two—when I got home. I thumbed through it and stopped at an article by David O. McKay. He talked about being the liaison between man and God—as he was the current prophet, seer, and revelator of the LDS Church. The next morning, I picked up my Bible and flopped it open. My eyes fell on 1 Timothy 2:5."

"Come on, Jim. You *flopped* open your Bible?"

"I'm telling you that's what happened."

"Okay. Okay, keep going."

"That verse says, 'For there is one God and one mediator between God and man, the man Christ Jesus.' I thought about the article by President McKay. Someone's got to be wrong. If there is only one God, then we can't become gods of our own planet as the church teaches. And if there's only one mediator, Christ Jesus, then the president of the church can't possibly be the go-between for us and God. It was then that I mentally left the church. And that's where I've been ever since. But I sure wasn't going to tell you."

"Whether you told me or not, Jim, God has been working on your heart and mine. This is not an accident."

Far into the night we talked, agreeing on each contradiction between what the church taught and what Jesus taught. It was as though God opened the floodgates and poured out His truth on us. I felt greatly relieved.

"It's so clear now," Jim said.

"So sudden," I agreed. "There's no way we can stay in the church any longer. What are we going to do?"

"I know one thing for sure," Jim added. "We're going to tell our friends right away so they won't get it second-hand."

"You mean like Greg and Linda?"

"Yes, especially Greg and Linda. With his being second counselor in the bishopric, he needs to know why we're making this decision. I'm sure he'll understand."

"I don't look forward to this, Jim. It's going to be tough."

"I know, but it's something we've got to do. We've made the decision, now we've got to act on it." We didn't even try to sleep. We were too excited. Adrenaline pumped non-stop, and joy filled our spirits that had been dry too long.

15

Emotional Turmoil

WHAT ABOUT PRIMARY? *It's so good for the kids. Maybe I can just let them continue going.* My thoughts whirled and then a twinge of anxiety gripped me. *I'm really going to miss Relief Society, too. I wonder if I can just attend and not believe?*

That evening Jim and I sat down on the floor facing each other. "What do you think about the kids?" I said. "How are we going to tell them?"

"Maybe we should let them make their own decision." Jim threw out the thought as though he were rolling dice. "On the other hand, that's pretty stupid. We're their parents. We make the decisions—they follow."

"Steve will soon be eleven and advance into the priesthood through the church's scouting program, Jim. And don't forget, Janet's going to be a teenager in two months and is president of her Merry Miss class. That's going to be tough. All their friends are Mormon. I don't think it will matter to Kirk, though. He's just four, so it won't make much difference to him. But they need to know what's going on with us. I don't think we should wait."

"You're right. Let's do it!"

"I'll go get the kids."

We gathered in the family room and Jim began.

"Kids, you need to sit down. Your mother and I have something very important to tell you." The whole story was unfolded before them during the next hour.

Questions, tears, and anger filled the air. "But I'm president of my Merry Miss class, Dad," Janet said with concern. "Will I have to drop out?"

"I won't get to go on scout outings anymore," Steve added. As preteens, it seemed more than they could bear.

"We're doing what we think is right, kids." I tried to assure our disbelieving children. "We've made the decision, but we're taking it one day at a time. We know it seems strange to you and tough to swallow, but your dad and I agree that, as a family, this is what we have to do. It's a decision you need to trust us on."

Jim and I ached for our kids and wanted to make it feel as right for them as it did for us. But I felt like a mother bird shoving her fledglings out of the nest. They would have to fly whether they wanted to or not. I didn't like being a mother bird.

———————

OUR NEXT STEP was a trip to the bishop's office the following day. We wanted the leaders to know the truth we'd discovered and not hear the story secondhand.

"Come in, Jim and Judy. Sit down." Bishop Nelson's

greeting was sugary sweet. "I'm glad to see you both. Now, what brings you here?"

"We're leaving the church, Bishop," Jim said without a blink. "There are teachings in the church that don't agree with what Jesus taught. Judy and I have been studying independently, and we've concluded that the doctrine of the LDS Church is from man and not God."

"Well, you know, I can't agree with that—but you have your free agency." The sound of the words was so familiar. I could practically have recited what he'd say next. "If you'll just study the *Book of Mormon*, you'll regain your testimony. Pray, and God will reveal the truth of it to you."

"Bishop Nelson, we've read the *Book of Mormon*." Jim clinched his jaw and waited a moment before continuing. "Although I don't have all the answers, it's clear to me that we can't become gods. That's the same lie the serpent presented to Eve!" Jim practically shouted.

"Not only that, but I found out we shouldn't do genealogies. At least not for the purpose of baptizing those who are already dead." Dan Nelson looked at me blankly.

"We couldn't rescue them anyway," I added. "Jesus invites sinners to accept Him as their atonement for sin here and now, not after they die. The doctrine of the church confuses people, Bishop." I felt my face flush. "It takes their eyes off Christ."

"Well, I'm not too worried about your confusion." Bishop Nelson leaned back in his chair and smiled a sideways grin. "Lots and lots of people question the church. But they always find their way back to it."

His confident air grated on me. I wanted to shout, "But

you don't understand!" It was obvious he had no intention of even trying to hear us out.

"You'll be back, too. I'm sure of it." Dan Nelson rose from his chair, all six feet of him, walked slowly to the door and held it open. We were dismissed as Primary children would have been.

As the door clicked shut behind us, Jim marched out ahead of me and slammed open the double glass doors hard with both hands. "He didn't even want to hear what we had to say!" Outside the ward building, Jim took a deep breath and sighed deeply.

"I am so disappointed, Jim. I thought he'd want to know why we were taking this drastic step. Do you think he'll tell Greg because he's in the bishopric?"

"I want our friends to hear it from us." Jim walked quickly to the car.

"Then we'll have to go tonight and tell them."

WE PULLED UP IN FRONT OF GREG AND LINDA'S house about 7:00 P.M. "I'm really not looking forward to this, Jim." I scooted across the seat to get out on Jim's side of the car.

"No need to worry, Judy. We know Greg and Linda. They'll understand."

"Guess we'll know soon," I whispered, and at the same time felt an urge to turn and run.

"Hi, Jim and Judy! Come right on in." Greg was a tall man in his early thirties. His wife, Linda, was equally as tall, and they dwarfed Jim and me.

"Glad to see you two. Have a seat." Linda was Relief Society president, and everyone's friend.

"We have something very serious we need to tell you two," Jim began, "and we don't want you to hear it from the grapevine." Jim paused, took a deep breath, and blurted, "We're leaving the church."

Linda stared at Jim, then at me, pressed her lips together and twisted in her seat. I thought she was going to leave the room, but she sat still and quiet.

Greg began with slow, measured words, "Well, Jim, whatever it is you're struggling with, I know you'll be back."

"Why do you say that, Greg?"

"Lots of people go through a period of questioning and, in the end, come back to the church." Greg continued, "Besides, Jim . . ." He paused. "Don't forget, you've been sealed in the temple, and I'm sure you enjoy sex."

Jim scooted to the edge of his seat. "What does *that* have to do with anything, Greg?"

"Only by honoring the covenants you made in the temple can you enjoy the bliss of married life for eternity."

"That sounds like bribery to me, Greg. And besides that, it has nothing to do with the decision we've made." Jim's face turned beet red.

"Don't you want to know the reasons we're leaving, Greg?" I asked.

"Not really. It doesn't matter. You'll be back."

"I'm sorry you don't want to hear what we've discovered." I looked at Linda. "You might be quite surprised." There was no response from her at all. It was as though her tongue was unable to move.

"Well, no need to stay any longer," Jim said as we rose from the couch in unison. We walked out of their living room and into the slightly cool desert night, dumbfounded.

I shook my head as we drove away. "They really didn't want to know our reasons for leaving, either, Jim."

"I just can't believe Greg tried to deal so dirty. What he alluded to was totally uncalled for," Jim replied.

"He sure embarrassed me!"

"I guess we just have to accept it and go on, Judy. Maybe this is the way it's going to be." We drove the rest of the way home in silence, trying to assimilate our friends' reactions.

We pulled to a stop in our carport. Tears began to well up in my eyes. "I never dreamed we'd be brushed off like that."

"Do you think any of our friends will ever listen, Judy?" Jim sat gripping the steering wheel.

"We've got to try to tell them, Jim. We've just got to try."

16

Desert Bonfire

AFTER WE TOLD THE LEADERS of the church of our decision to leave, the news spread quickly through the families of the ward. Janet, who'd just entered junior high, came home from school and slammed her books down.

"I'll never belong to another church again as long as I live!" She threw herself down on the family room couch and crossed her arms over her chest.

I sat down beside her and put my arm around her. "What happened?" I said quietly.

"Denise, Kim, Terri, and Kathy all ganged up on me in PE and demanded to know why I left the church. Even my PE teacher quizzed me." Janet brushed my arm from her shoulder. "I told them I don't know why we left the stupid church—we just *did*!"

Her words shot through me like a hot poker. *What have I done to my daughter?* I cried out to God silently, *Oh, God, help us get through this!*

No words could soothe the sting left from the drilling

Janet received from her friends. She had no answers for them—that's what hurt most. She didn't know how to respond. Neither Jim nor I had answers either. We knew we had to get out of the Mormon Church, and we knew we wanted Jesus' way and not man's, but we were at a loss as to how to go about it. It was little help for our daughter, who, at one of the most vulnerable times of her life, was rejected by her peers.

There was shunning even from Steve's Primary friends. "My friends won't play with me anymore, Mom." Families were afraid their children would begin asking questions, too. It was safer to stay away from the Robertsons.

My close friend and neighbor, Donna, came to see me. "Judy, do you know what you're losing by leaving the church?" Tears streamed down her face.

"Donna, don't cry for me. Save your tears for those who don't know the Lord." It seemed a rather pious statement, but that's the way I felt. I wasn't losing anything. I had, in fact, gained the most important treasure in my life—Jesus. I sensed His presence now. Even though I was saddened by our friends' reactions, there was a deep-down peace that was inexplicable. I knew Donna wouldn't understand. I hadn't understood, either, until now.

"You'll no longer have the blessings of the priesthood in your family or the protection of your garments, you know. Oh Judy, there are so many other things you'll lose. Please reconsider. Don't do this!"

"Donna, I appreciate your concern for me, but I have not made this decision lightly. It's firm; we're leaving the church."

David Jackson, Joe's father and a regional representative of the church, called and asked if he could pay us a visit. He said he would like to bring his son, who was a state senator, and Joe, too. "Looks like they're bringing the big guns, Jim. Are you ready for this?"

"Guess I'll have to be."

———

THAT EVENING THE THREE CAME OVER. The tension in the air was thick. "Judy, Jim, you know how we all love you. We're extremely sad to hear you're having problems with the church. Is there anyone who has hurt you?"

"No, David, no one has hurt us. We are leaving the church for doctrinal reasons, not because of anything anyone has said or done. We no longer believe the LDS Church is true."

"Is there anything we can do to change your minds? Any questions we can answer for you?"

"We appreciate your concern, but there is nothing you can do. We've made up our minds." The three men gave Jim and me a hug as they left. We felt the loss of friendship as they walked out our door, but we were firm in our decision.

The next day I had to take care of another final leaving— as Cub Scout den mother. I knew I could no longer hold that position in the Mormon Church. I needed to cut ties completely.

I drove up to the ward building and parked as Jim and I had done a few days before. This time I would have to face the bishop alone.

"Come in, come in, Judy," Bishop Nelson greeted me. He seemed unusually warm.

"Bishop, I want to resign as Cub Scout den mother. Since we've decided to leave the church, it would not be fair for me to hold this position."

"Judy, I'm not worried about you holding this position. But there is something else I'm concerned about. Jim is leading you down a rocky path. Are you sure you want to follow him?"

"Bishop, in the first place, Jim is not leading me. I made my own decision that the church was not true. I'm not doing this blindly. I know full well what I'm doing. It's my personal decision to leave the church."

"I just want you to know there are alternatives. You don't have to follow Jim any longer. He no longer holds the priesthood." A sick feeling filled my stomach. I felt an urgency to leave, to get out of the presence of this man who was suggesting things I didn't even want to think about and questioning my own and Jim's integrity to boot.

"You will have to find a replacement for me for the Cub Scouts, Dan." It sounded funny to call him by his first name, but it helped reality sink in for him, too. He was no longer my bishop. This was it. It was final.

I left quickly. I felt strongly that he wanted me to stay and discuss the matter further. I wanted no part of a conspiracy to undermine Jim or to separate from him. Jim and I were finally together on our decision after a year of friction. We had faced the reality that we had been involved in an immense deception all these years. We would deal with it together, with the help of God, not separately.

The "testimony," repeated over and over by members on Fast and Testimony Sunday, rolled through my head. The voices of children saying, *"I know the church is true and that Joseph Smith is a prophet of God"* played like a tape recording over and over in my mind. *"The church is true . . . the church is true."*

I felt like screaming, "The church is *not* true!"

I ran to the car. *I must get out of here quick. I don't even like the feeling of this place anymore.*

T HAT EVENING JIM AND I DISCUSSED the difficulty the kids were having. "It would be easier to stay LDS, Jim. Not that I want to. It's just that the pressure the kids are experiencing is getting me down."

"We've got to take a drastic step," he said. "I was thinking as I drove home from work, we need to get rid of everything that is Mormon."

"What do you mean, Jim?"

"I mean get rid of all our books, our garments, anything that connects us to the church. Take them to a dump or something. I want it all out of our house."

"Maybe we should burn it, then. We don't want anyone else to have it, do we?"

"You're right. If it's useless stuff, we certainly don't want others to go through what we have. Let's just pile it all in the pickup and take it to the desert. We'll find a place where we can set fire to it and be rid of it once and for all— get it out of our lives forever."

"I'll gather it all while you're at work tomorrow."

E ACH BOOK I PLACED IN THE BOX held special meaning—time spent on some project. Relief Society home-teaching manual, hours spent visiting LDS homes to see about their welfare; Primary books, untold hours teaching young children the good moral characteristics of the Mormon prophets; songbooks; family home evening manuals; food storage instruction; and the lessons on family exaltation and genealogies, the ones that caused the deep questions in my mind.

By evening, I had an amazing amount of paraphernalia loaded in boxes. It gave me an opportunity to show the kids some of the reasons we no longer believed as we had. I opened the LDS hymnbook and scanned the lines of a couple of hymns. I told the kids that "O My Father" speaks of preexistence and a heavenly mother. "Praise to the Man" includes the words, "Great is his glory and endless his priesthood. . . . Hail to the Prophet. . . . Mingling with God's. . . ."[1] "It glorifies Joseph Smith instead of Jesus," I said. "We believe only the Bible to be the true Word of God. These teachings are the opposite of what His Word reveals to us."

O KAY, WE'RE READY." We loaded the stuff, including our garments, into the pickup and drove out to the desert.

"This looks like a good spot in this dry wash," Jim said. We all jumped out and began unloading the truck. After Jim lit the fire, he stood examining a leather-bound copy of the Standard Works with our names engraved in gold lettering. "I hate to burn this. It was a gift from the Jacksons." But he shook his head and threw it onto the fire.

Seven years of our lives ended with gray smoke billowing up from the leather-bound copy and a snap and popping sound as more paper and books caught fire. I sat with my arms around my knees, staring at the dancing flames.

"You know, Jim, I feel as though a big, heavy load is lifting from my shoulders and going up in that smoke." Soon crackling yellow flames engulfed the whole pile of lies, and the pungent odor of black smoke stung our nostrils.

"This symbolizes we're starting our lives anew," I said to the children. "No longer will we follow the ways of man. We will serve God alone." We sat watching the embers slowly fade.

Steve, our Boy Scout, poured water over the charred remains. Clear, fresh water washed over the blackness that we'd all been involved in.

The backbreaking weight of Mormonism lay in a pile of ashes. We were free of its laws and ordinances and could now set our faces toward replacing it all with the gift of grace and mercy through Jesus Christ.

We bowed our heads, and Jim said a simple, heartfelt prayer for us all. "God, help us to know what to do now. How do we serve you and not be led astray again?"

I WROTE MY FAMILY about our decision:

> Mom and Dad,
>
> Now that we realize what we were involved in all these years, I'm asking you to forgive me for any hurt I caused the family because of our beliefs. I hope you will understand. I also want to thank you for raising me in a Christian home. Dad, thank you for reading Bible stories to us kids when we were little. I'm trying to find a Bible storybook for our kids, like the one you read to us.

My dad wrote that he was very happy about our decision and was praying the Lord would guide us into a church. One month later, my dad died. The travel back to Arkansas brought back a flood of memories both good and bad. But mostly I thanked God that He had opened my eyes before my dad died.

When I arrived at my parents' home, my mom handed me a Bible storybook—just like the one Dad had read to me as a child. He had looked hard to find it, Mom said. He wrote in the front of it:

> To Jim and Judy. Enjoy many hours of reading to Janet, Steve, and Kirk. Love, Dad

17

Dawn at Usery Pass

HOW MUCH FARTHER, DAD?" Kirk puffed out his question. "This mountain is too big. Can't we stop now?"

"We're almost there, son." Jim held Kirk's hand as Janet and Steve ran ahead to a high point overlooking the Phoenix valley.

"Let's stop here, Jim. There are some smooth places to sit on these boulders. The sun's coming up fast. It'll be hot soon."

We all found our own special rock and watched the rays of gold mingle with the clear-blue eastern sky. We had come to this same spot for five Sundays.

"It's so quiet up here," Kirk said.

"It's Sunday, remember?" Steve informed his kid brother.

"We don't have a church to go to now, guys, so your mom and I decided we'd come here, to our favorite picnic spot, and have our own church service." Jim seemed more relaxed than I'd seen him in some time. "We're going to read the Bible and pray, and we'll come to this spot every Sunday just like we were going to a church building. What do you think about that?"

"I love it out here at Usery Mountain." Steve caught a cricket and played with it.

"Seems kind of weird to me," Janet mumbled under her breath. "Nobody I know goes to a mountain for church with just their family." Janet flicked long strands of blond hair out of her eyes.

"I know it's different, Janet," Jim assured his skeptical daughter. "But we're going to try this for a while. Our family needs time together."

"Okay, let's pray," Jim said abruptly. Janet, Steve, and Kirk folded their arms. *Father in heaven, it's beautiful here, and we're glad we're all together. We need you. Please lead us. In Jesus' name, Amen.*

"Kids, you don't have to fold your arms anymore," I said as gently as possible. "I know you learned that's what you're supposed to do in Primary and Sunday school, but we want to do things differently now. Just close your eyes when we pray, and that's enough, okay?"

"Hon, read something in the Bible for us, will you?" We were all so casual and relaxed, it somehow didn't seem like it would "take."

"I'll start in Psalms. It's right in the middle of the Bible." I put both my thumbs in the center of my King James Bible and pulled it open. "I think that's where we are right now, in a way. We're not in Mormonism anymore, but we're not anywhere else either. We're in the middle."

I began reading Psalm 1:

Blessed is the man that walketh not in the counsel of the ungodly, nor standeth in the way of sinners, nor sitteth in the seat of the scornful. But his delight is in the law of the Lord; and in his law doth he meditate day and night. And he shall be like a tree planted by the rivers of water, that bringeth forth his fruit in his season; his leaf also shall not wither; and whatsoever he doeth shall prosper. The ungodly are not so: but are like the chaff which the wind driveth away. Therefore the ungodly shall not stand in the judgment, nor sinners in the congregation of the righteous. For the Lord knoweth the way of the righteous: but the way of the ungodly shall perish.

The sound of a soft breeze rustling through nearby paloverde trees and the sight of a hawk gliding on thermals gave us a sense of being far out in the wilderness, and yet we were only ten miles from our home in Mesa.

"Are we ever going to a church again?" Kirk asked.

We sat in silence for a few minutes. Then Jim sighed. "What do you all think? Should we try to find another church?"

Steve shrugged his shoulders. Janet stared out over the high desert landscape.

"Why don't we ask God?" I suggested.

"Good idea, hon. Go for it."

"Father, we need your help. We've been in the Mormon Church now for seven years. It's not what we thought it was. It's a church built around man's ideas. We don't know where to turn now. Could you please lead us to a church that honors you and your Word?"

SUNDAY, THE DAY OF REST, was another good thing we learned in the Mormon Church. But we realized the good things didn't balance out the false things we were taught.

The quietness emphasized the big void inside us. All our friends were Mormon, but none of them wanted anything to do with us now. We needed others to help us through this time. We didn't know where to turn.

Usery Pass filled a need as we huddled together—the five of us—seeking to find God in our turmoil. Jumping directly back into a church was not the first step we needed to take. Identifying the longings of our hearts was first. Sometimes it takes foolish things to bring us to where we need to be. Dawn arrived in our hearts as the sun rose on us that Sunday morning in the desert.

LOUNGING ON OUR LIVING ROOM COUCH that Sunday afternoon, I reflected. "Jim, let's call John and Lorene Maguire in Arkansas. Remember how John and his son asked us about our relationship with Christ before we left for Arizona?"

"Let's do it!" Jim picked up the phone and dialed.

"John! This is Jim Robertson. I called to tell you and Lorene that Judy and I have left the Mormon Church."

"Praise the Lord! Jim, it's so good to hear from you." John turned his head from the phone and yelled, "Lorene, get on the phone quick!"

"We wanted you two to be the first to know. You and Lorene have always meant so much to us even though we haven't been in touch for seven years. We made a big mistake joining the LDS Church."

"Well, Jim, there's no time like today to make a decision for the Lord."

"We've been praying for the two of you for seven years," Lorene added. "What good news. But where are you going to church now?"

"We're not going anywhere right now, Lorene," I said. "But we're asking God to guide us. We've been having our own church—just the five of us."

"You need friendship with other Christians, Judy."

"We're finding that out. Our kids need friends and so do we."

———

TALKING TO OLD FRIENDS gave us courage to take steps to find a church. How to go about that was the dilemma.

"I'm going to take a look in the Yellow Pages," I said, dragging down our East Valley directory. "I don't have a clue where to start looking, though. There are more LDS churches in here than anything else. I know this sounds weird, but there's a church here named *Central*. Doesn't that mean 'middle'? Remember when I read from the middle of the Bible this morning and said that's where we are, right in the middle—not Mormon, but not anything else either? It's listed under *Christian*. Maybe that would be safe. Should we try it?"

"Guess it won't hurt to try." Jim came to look over my shoulder. "We've got to be careful. It has to center on Jesus, on the Bible, and nothing else. How are we going to know?"

"We asked God to direct us. So I think He will."

———

THE NEXT SUNDAY, we drove to the little church we'd found in the Yellow Pages.

"Jim, I'm scared to go into this place." We held hands as we walked up to the small white-framed building. "What if it's another church like the Mormon Church? How in the world will we know?"

"This is scary to me, too, Judy. I don't want to make another mistake," Jim said, squeezing my hand. "But we've just got to go in and see what it's like."

We slipped into the sanctuary and scooted into the back row as the people were standing up to sing a hymn. My palms were sweaty and my heart beat rapidly. I hoped no one would turn around and look at us. *I wish we could be invisible,* I thought.

It had been such a long time since I'd been to a regular church. *Will I remember the hymns? Will we have to introduce ourselves?*

The pastor began to read his Bible text for his sermon. His voice was strong, assured, and soothing to my pent-up emotions:

> I am amazed that you are so quickly deserting Him who called you by the grace of Christ, for a different gospel; which is really not another; only there are some who are disturbing you, and want to distort the gospel

of Christ. But even though we, or an angel from heaven, should preach to you a gospel contrary to that which we have preached to you, let him be accursed. As we have said before, so I say again now, if any man is preaching to you a gospel contrary to that which you received, let him be accursed. (Galatians 1:6–9, *NASB*)

The Bible-reading startled me. I felt as though the pastor was directing it to us. We had deserted God and followed a false gospel. *Does this pastor know ex-Mormons are here? But how could he?*

I was stunned that the sermon seemed tailor-made for us. How could he have known we were there? It didn't occur to me that Charles Cook didn't know we were there, but God did, and He was using this servant of His to speak to us right where we were.

We were in need of repentance from following a false gospel. We needed to turn to the God of our lives, who created us and gave us His Son to atone for our rebellion against Him.

How gracious God is. Thank you for leading us here today, I prayed silently. I felt a sense of peace again. I had let God in to speak to my heart. Yes, He was guiding us. Yes, He did care about the details of our lives. We had asked for guidance, and He had given it.

We slipped out of the pew and shook hands at the front door with this pastor who had opened God's Word to us. My fear melted as he shook my hand warmly and thanked us for coming. *This man has no idea who we are. But I've never before felt such warmth emanate from a person. He truly cares that we came.*

"Jim, I want to go back there," I said as he started the car.

"So do I." We drove home in silence, both of us deep in thought.

T URNING TO THE YELLOW PAGES may not be the best way to search for a church, but we didn't know the way. In our ignorance, God led us and gave us the quiet time we needed to process all that we had been through. I was about to find out how deep the love of God is, who pursued us even when we walked away from Him.

18

Grace So Amazing

THE CUP OF STEAMING COFFEE sat in front of me on the kitchen table. *It's like a witch's brew enticing me,* I thought. *I'm not sure I should drink this stuff.* I took a sip and set the cup down, feeling somewhat guilty. The Mormon Church had taught us that drinking coffee was bad for the body. We should abstain from it as well as alcohol and tobacco. This revelation was called the Word of Wisdom. It was revealed to Joseph Smith and written in the *Doctrine and Covenants* as an ordinance. In fact, the "church" used it as one of the measuring rods to see if its members were worthy to have a temple recommend.

I wanted to complete my Bible study before the kids got up. I had joined a class at our new church called Memorize the Word. We took three verses per week and read them in context, cross-referenced them, told how they applied to our lives today, and then repeated them to ourselves each day. At the end of the week, we repeated the verses to a partner in the class.

My verse was Colossians 2:8 from the King James version of the Bible: "Beware lest any man spoil you through philosophy and vain deceit, after the tradition of men, after the rudiments of the world, and not after Christ."

"Jim!" I yelled to my husband in the back of the house. "You've got to read this one. It's written just for us!"

"I was just coming to show you a verse, too." He handed me his open Bible. "Read this." He pointed to Galatians 2:16: "Knowing that a man is not justified by the works of the law, but by the faith of Jesus Christ, even we have believed in Jesus Christ, that we might be justified by the faith of Christ, and not by the works of the law: for by the works of the law shall no flesh be justified" (KJV).

"See?" Jim thumped his Bible. "That means us. Keeping all kinds of laws and ordinances gets us nowhere."

"I know, I know, but you've got to see the rest of this chapter in Colossians. It says we are 'complete in Him,' and look at this in verse 20: "Why, as though living in the world, are ye subject to ordinances, (Touch not; taste not; handle not; Which all are to perish with the using;) after the commandments and doctrines of men? Which things have indeed a shew of wisdom in will worship, and humility, and neglecting of the body; not in any honor to the satisfying of the flesh" (Colossians 2:20–23).

"It says it better here in the *New International Version*": "Such regulations indeed have an appearance of wisdom, with their self-imposed worship, their false humility and their harsh treatment of the body, but they lack any value in restraining sensual indulgence" (Colossians 2:23).

"I can't tell you how much that gives me a sense of freedom," I said. "I can drink this coffee and not feel guilty at all. It's not abstaining from this stuff that makes me righteous, anyway; it's faith in Jesus Christ! Wow!" I jumped up from the table. "I'm really free!"

"Kids, get up!" I called as I ran down the hall. "It's time to get ready for school."

AN AD IN THE SUNDAY CHURCH BULLETIN caught my eye: Bill Gothard's "Institute in Basic Youth Conflicts," a week-long conference for families. The advertisement described how participants would learn to apply Scripture in dealing with conflicts that occur in their lives.

I was most concerned about Janet. After leaving the Mormon Church, our daughter struggled. This week-long conference looked like it could be a tool in helping us cope with her and help her deal with the pressures of a world that offered all kinds of juicy enticements to a thirteen-year-old.

At our kitchen table, I prayed for guidance in a new way. "Lord, we're having a tough time relating to Janet as she goes through what I know is a natural teenage rebellion. The Basic Youth Conflicts conference may be just what we need. It costs fifty-five dollars to register our family; we don't have the extra cash right now, Lord. But if this is something that will help Janet, and us, would you provide the funds for it?"

I left the kitchen and walked toward the kids' bedrooms. As I passed by the hall closet, the thought struck me: *The 100-pound sack of pinto beans! They're selling for eighty-five dollars right now. Dry-food stores might buy them from us!*

As soon as the kids left the house for school, I grabbed

the Yellow Pages again and looked up "Food Storage." There were several outlets that served the large LDS population in Mesa.

All LDS families were supposed to maintain a year's supply of food and essentials on hand at all times. (In later years, it was suggested that families keep a two-year supply.) This was taught as "family preparedness" in case of natural disaster or job loss.

I began with the first store. "I have a 100-pound sack of pinto beans. Would you be interested in purchasing them—for eighty-five dollars?"

"No, we're not interested."

Not to be discouraged on the first phone call, I continued down the food storage list.

"I have 100 pounds of pinto beans I won't be needing. Would you be interested in buying them for seventy-five dollars?"

"No, we're not interested."

I lowered the price to sixty-five on the third call and was refused again. Then I offered the dried beans to a fourth store for fifty-five dollars.

"Yes, we'll buy them. Bring them down."

Thank you, Lord. Guess I was being a bit greedy.

This proved to be a powerful faith-building incident for me and only the first of many evidences of His tenderness in the days to follow.

JANET SAT BETWEEN JIM AND ME at the week-long seminar. It was a time of healing for us as we found scriptural ways to deal with tough issues plaguing our daughter and us. Janet, a teenager, and Steve, a preteen, needed boundaries. Kirk, just four, needed guidance, too, and this seminar was one of many tools God supplied that seemed tailor-made for the difficulties we were experiencing.

Then we attended a Billy Graham Crusade at the Arizona State University stadium. What a moving experience for us all. Our daughter, who sat with a friend from church, went forward that night and accepted Christ into her life.

At a Sunday morning worship service, Janet and Steve were baptized by the youth pastor, who had been teaching them what it meant to be a follower of Christ. I sat at the back of the church watching this drama take place.

"In the likeness of Christ's death," Tom Hawks said, gently laying our son backward into the water, "and of His resurrection." His tender-but-clear voice was like a tolling bell to me as he lifted Steve out of the water. He gave Steve a bear hug before he left the pool to make way for his sister to enter.

The simple beauty of this momentous event was reenacted a second time as Janet was immersed. The scene blurred through my tear-filled eyes.

At that moment, it hit me hard. As Mormons, we had been leading our children away from the Lord. So much time was spent in the Mormon Church cleaning up our outward lives. But we failed in the most important aspect: examining our own hearts.

We had followed a "wolf," who nearly destroyed our little flock. But the Good Shepherd heard the bleating of the weakest sheep and rescued us. He not only answered my pinto-bean prayer, He answered prayers I hadn't even prayed.

"Which of you, if his son asks for bread, will give him a stone? Or if he asks for a fish, will give him a snake? If you, then, though you are evil, know how to give good gifts to your children, how much more will your Father in heaven give good gifts to those who ask him!" (Matthew 7:9–11).

Part Four

My Life After Mormonism

19

Religious Refugees

LIKE A CIRCUS BARKER, I wanted to call out to every Mormon I knew, "Look, look what I found out! The church is not true! See the unveiled truth about Joseph Smith—he was a charlatan! Examine the discrepancies we found in the *Book of Mormon*, the *Doctrine and Covenants*, and the *Pearl of Great Price*. Scrutinize the history and learn: No bones have ever been excavated from the Hill Cumorah!

"Risk! I know you've been told to ignore literature that's not faith promoting, but you *must* listen to the oaths you repeat in the temple! Remember the chants at the veil! You're committing yourself to Lucifer! Get out! Get out before it's too late!"

This was my fantasy. I wanted to shake every Mormon I came in contact with and remove the blinders from their eyes. I felt overwhelmed with concern for my former friends who were still Latter-day Saints. They were drowning in a pit of lies. At the very least, they were wearing themselves out trying to earn their way to the Celestial Kingdom in a man-made religion. But most important, they were missing out on the grace and mercy given to us freely through Jesus. I felt compassion for them and wanted them to experience the same joy that I now had. But they were still stuck in bondage to a cruel taskmaster. *I've got to help them out! I have the truth; I want them to have it, too!*

"Oh, I want so badly for them to know, God!" I cried out. "I beg you, let me tell them!"

WE TOOK THE PAPER with our written testimony and a few of the comparisons of Mormon doctrine and the Bible to the friends who introduced us to Mormonism in the first place. The sun sank quietly behind the San Tan Mountains as we pulled up to Joe and Ellen's house in the desert southwest of Queen Creek. "Can you hear my heart pounding, Jim?"

"It's just Joe and Ellen, honey. Don't worry, they'll understand."

"Jim, I don't think they will, but we've got to try and tell them. Joe has never known anything but Mormonism. And once Ellen married Joe, she sold out to everything Mormon. It wouldn't surprise me if they chased us out of their home."

Jim held my sweaty hand as we walked up to Joe and Ellen's sprawling ranch-style home. Joe opened the door. "Come on in, Jim and Judy. It's good to see you. Sit down."

Small talk came abruptly to an end, and Jim began, "Guess you've been wondering why we left the church." Joe crossed his arms and Ellen leaned back on the couch. "We wanted you to know exactly why we made the decision we did."

The stillness made me uncomfortable as Jim handed our typewritten testimony to Joe. "We hope you'll read the discrepancies we've uncovered in our research, Joe and Ellen. We didn't leave because we were unhappy with anyone in the church. We left for doctrinal reasons—some of which we have listed here." Jim pointed to the paper resting on Joe's knee.

Joe and Ellen stared blankly at the paper. Silence hovered over the room as though we were in a forest stalking the big cat that stared at us from a framed picture above their heads.

I want them to know the truth so badly, Lord. Just as badly as they wanted us to know about Mormonism when we first met them. But the silence screamed their answer.

"Joe and Ellen, we treasure you as our friends." A lump blocked the words in my throat and my voice squeaked. "We have nothing to hide, and when the time is right, we want to talk with you about the reasons we made our decision. But we'll leave that up to you."

We drove home physically weak, reflecting on the shouted-but-unspoken words: *We really don't want to know. We are happy being LDS. It's a shame you've left the only true church. You've made your choice. Now go.*

AN EPIDEMIC OF CURIOSITY infected our Sunday school class. Jim and I were asked if we would lead a question-and-answer session the following Sunday. Some members of our class lived next door to Mormons, some worked with them or for them; some even had LDS relatives.

Jim and I compiled some of the Mormon beliefs and made comparisons with historic Christianity. We researched the history of Mormonism, contrasted Mormon beliefs with Bible references, and presented this information to our Sunday school class.

Our community has a high percentage of Mormons. "What makes them tick?" they wanted to know.

"Why are LDS seminary buildings across the street from every junior and senior high school in the state of Arizona? Why is their Institute of Religion across the street from Mesa Community College? What goes on in the temple?"

The questions were endless.

Most had a gut feeling there was something wrong with the LDS Church, but they didn't know what it was. After all, it was so enticing: the clean, well-manicured lawns, the wholesome family image.

"What generates such fierce devotion in their church?"

None of their questions could be answered in three short sentences or less. "Who is behind the concept of Mormonism? Why is it so appealing?"

In response to these questions, Jim and I had to come to terms with some issues in our own lives: "How were you lured into Mormonism?" we were asked. "Didn't you study the Bible?"

"Well, no, we didn't. We were vulnerable to the beautiful package the LDS Church presents. Its members are the finest people you'll ever meet."

NEW FRIENDS AND ACQUAINTANCES referred hurting friends to us—friends whose sons or daughters had joined the LDS Church, or relatives who were re-thinking their membership. I listened intently and hurt with them. I showed them verses from the Bible I'd found that expose the LDS doctrine as a counterfeit.

Each time Jim unveiled our story—how we became Mormon and why we left—eyes lit up; confusion vanished. There was hope after all. Maybe they could help their loved ones see this, too, as we had.

No amount of money could buy the deep joy Jim and I felt as each individual visited us. In fact, many times after a session, usually in the evening, we would go for a drive, waiting for the rush of adrenaline to subside so we could go home and sleep.

We couldn't have known what lay ahead for our lives, but God did. He had a plan, and it was about to be unveiled to us.

"Turn you at my reproof: behold, I will pour out my spirit unto you, I will make known my words unto you" (Proverbs 1:23 KJV).

20

The Molding of a Ministry

J UDY, THERE'S A COUPLE who live across the street from us. Mormon missionaries visited them, and they're confused. Would you be willing to talk to them?" Joe and Toni, two new friends from church, asked.

"Sure, we'll talk to them—and tell them what we went through."

W HY ISN'T SOMEONE DOING SOMETHING about this?" Beth fumed after our presentation. "They almost sold us on their church. I've never heard about this religion, ever, in church."

"The Mormon Church seems to have it all together," Chet retorted.

"Yes, that's what we thought, too." Jim added, "That's why we joined. It looks great on the outside. But the deep teachings of the Mormon Church are not taught to the public. You only find that out once you're firmly entrenched in the culture."

The more we talked with Beth and Chet Smith, the more it became apparent there was a need to educate the Christian community about the subtle deceit of Mormonism.

"Judy and Jim, do you know anyone else who might be interested in forming a group to help squelch this spread of Mormonism?" Beth was not about to sit back and do nothing.

"Yes, we do know others who would be interested," I assured her.

"Why don't we meet next Thursday and discuss what can be done?" I sensed urgency in Beth's voice. "We can meet at our house," she added.

I made a list of those who had expressed interest in helping and called them.

About eight of us gathered in Chet and Beth's living room the following week. Beth told us that she had queried everyone she knew: "Do y'all know about these Mormon people?" she asked in her soft southern accent.

They all said, "It's no big deal. Mormons live all around us. We don't think too much of it."

Beth was incensed. "Well, why don't you? Don't you know they're a cult?"

"How can you call Mormonism a cult?" Beth's neighbor asked. "These people are good-hearted and sincere. They *live* their religion. We as Christians could learn a lot from them."

Beth sat on the edge of the couch at our first meeting. "We must do something about this. Everyone I talked to thinks Mormonism is just another Christian denomination, or an offbeat church at worst. It's not a big deal to them. We must let people know the seriousness of what the Mormon Church is."

Bob Johnson, who had previously lived and worked among Mormons in Salt Lake City, chimed in, "Beth is right. Very few people are aware that the Latter-day Saints are a false religion, and its members are kept out of the arms of Jesus by its Old Testament-type laws and ordinances. Joseph Smith made sure of that with the false doctrine and volumes of so-called revelations he espoused. Mormons put him right up there next to God. Did you know they believe a person has to have Joseph Smith's consent to receive salvation? It's a culture unto itself. And in Utah, you're an alien if you're not Mormon."

Our pastor, Charles Cook, and John Hendee, the minister of Christian education from our church, listened intently. "Our people need to be trained in the subtle techniques Mormons use to draw people in," Charles said.

John agreed. "We need effective ways to educate Christians."

Doris Gurtler's daughter, Kim, had dated a Mormon boy, and wanted to know what to say to him now that he was on his mission. (See Glossary, p. 204, Missionaries.)

"We all have deep concerns," Charles said. "Let's pray and ask God for direction."

We met weekly to pray and formulate our goals and strategy. We named our group Concerned Christians, identifying as our primary concern the issue of the effect of Mormonism on the body of Christ.

Our twofold purpose evolved: Teach the Christian community through literature and public forums, and inform Mormons about the differences between Mormonism and historical Christianity. We outlined a book and began research.

There was another need we hadn't yet identified. Through mutual acquaintances, we met Bob Witte, an ex-Mormon and now a Christian. He knew others who had also left for doctrinal reasons. He, too, had done a significant amount of research. "Let's get together and compare notes."

Bob and his wife, Karen, lived in North Phoenix. They had moved to Arizona from Illinois, and Bob had formed an Ex-Mormons for Jesus group with another ex-Mormon named Melaine Layton. Instant bonding occurred between this couple and us.

"We're kindred spirits," Bob said. "What we were taught in the 'church' is not true." He went on, "The only people who leave Mormonism are not those who have moral problems and can't live up to the laws and ordinances of the church. There are many LDS that question the doctrine as we did. They didn't go down the tubes, either, as we were told by the 'church.'"

We chatted on and on into the night. We had a connection—a line of communication with others who'd gone through the same thing we had. We felt relieved; a burden lifted as we shared. We were no longer alone. Bob called it a "spiritual Alcoholics Anonymous."

Meeting others and talking about our shared experiences somehow spread a healing balm over wounds that, before now, defied complete healing. Other ex-LDS could use this kind of help, too. There was a great need for a support group, and Concerned Christians could meet this need.

"Let's take out a classified ad in the *Mesa Tribune* and see what happens." I suggested.

"Why not?"

The ad read: *We're searching for others who have left the LDS Church and seek fellowship with those of similar background. Write us in care of* Mesa Tribune, *Box 88. All inquiries held in strict confidence.*

Ex-Mormons responded to the newspaper ad and dared to come to a meeting at our home. They shared their experiences, and we gave encouragement.

More and more hurting people attended. We had all been through difficult times. We prayed with the ones who expressed a need for healing in their lives or who felt a desire to touch loved ones. Each session was much like an Alcoholics Anonymous meeting, only for ex-Latter-day Saints.

We opened God's Word at these meetings, worked through various LDS doctrines, and replaced them with the truth. Often we heard, "No one ever told me before how much Jesus loves me."

We guided the refugees into various Bible-based, Christ-centered churches in the valley. No certain denomination was pushed. We searched out fellowships for them in the areas where they lived, calling on pastors to introduce them, draw them in, and nurture them.

Every Christian church, no matter what the name, as long as it held the Bible alone as the only infallible Word of God and Jesus as Savior and Lord, received a refugee from Mormonism to nurture and care for.

We noticed a pattern in our meetings. Those who had attended for about six weeks learned the differences between Mormonism and Christianity, and the process of healing began. They moved on and involved themselves in a local church. A few stayed to help newcomers. New ones came every week. Those who had never been Mormon, but were touched in some way by its influence, were like cheerleaders. They were there for those who were hurting, helping in any way they could.

Soon our group was asked to speak and hold seminars at various churches. A need was identified: Church members were ill-equipped to deal with the strong appeal of Mormonism. Teenagers were being drawn in, or other relatives. Many worked with and for the LDS or lived in Mormon neighborhoods.

"What do I do when I am invited to a Mormon activity? My son plays basketball at the LDS ward next to our house." Most were concerned, but didn't know what to do about it.

Jim and I knew, because we had been there. Other ex-LDS knew, too, and we shared our experiences and our ever-increasing knowledge of the differences between Mormonism and Christianity. We went wherever and whenever we were invited to speak, and one speaking engagement led to another.

Individuals typically stormed the speaker after the session with questions: "My daughter joined the LDS Church. What do I do now?" People came to us with various problems they had encountered with Mormons. "As Christians, what is the right thing to do?"

The body of Christ needed protection from Mormonism's alluring wave. Christians who believed in the Bible, but didn't really know what it said, were caught up in its wake. The clean-cut, righteous appearance of the Mormon people pulled hundreds of unprepared Christians into the depths of their religion.

Families stood by helplessly, not knowing how to rescue floundering loved ones. Heartache descended upon their lives without warning. We sat with and listened to those with emotions battered, spirits bruised, and minds brainwashed. We were told of cruel counsel: "Divorce your husband; he's leading you down a rocky path. Marry a good LDS man who can take you to the temple." Indeed, many of us had experienced this counsel, too.

Paralyzing fear overcame most when they attempted to leave the church. Where does this kind of fear come from? James Fraser put it well in his biography, *Mountain Rain*, in speaking of a people he attempted to convert to Christianity:

> The "strong man" has not yet been bound, if I may put it so. The majority of the people are too afraid of their demons to turn to God as yet.

Those who have renounced Mormonism must also remove the chains that bind them to this "strong man." Sometimes this takes the form of destroying or taking off the paraphernalia of the false religion, but, most important, the putting on of the full armor of Christ—His Word.

G OD DIRECTED TO OUR MEETINGS those who were bruised and battered by the false teachings of Mormonism. He allowed us to open floodgates of emotion in innumerable hurting individuals and to provide the ointment of God's Word to their wounds, allowing them to accept the love Jesus offered.

I WANTED SO DESPERATELY to tell my Mormon friends, "Get out. Get out before it's too late." But God had another plan for Jim and me. He wanted to use us to warn others: "Beware! Mormonism is a slick counterfeit religion."

He wanted us to be there for those who had battle scars from the effects of Mormonism in their lives. He opened the door for countless hours on the phone and in our home, listening to hurting religious refugees. We offered the healing words of Jesus, encouraged them to read God's Word, and directed them to a local church near them. This was only the beginning of a ministry that neither Jim nor I could have ever thought possible.

21

Anonymous Benefactor

I OPENED SEVERAL PIECES of mail I'd just retrieved from our box, when I noticed one without a return address. *Odd. Who would send a letter like this?*

I sliced open the top and found inside a two-page typed letter and a cashier's check. I scanned the contents quickly. My mouth dropped open in disbelief. I handed the letter to Jim. "You've got to read this!"

> July 16, 1979
> Dear M/M Robertson:
>
> Inasmuch as my introduction to your group involved the discussion of your conversion from Mormonism to Christianity, I have taken the liberty of addressing this letter to your care.
>
> In this world, all great achievements are the result of humble beginnings, combined with perseverance and guided by the Word of God. As I understand it, the Concerned Christians group is at this point in its infancy and humble beginnings; but what it lacks in

numbers, it makes up for through its relentless pursuit of God's children who have been spiritually blinded by Mormonism.

One area your group is involved in, which is of particular interest to me, is the booklet you are developing on how to witness to a Mormon. Its description leads me to believe it is a tool to be used by the lay Christian. I feel very strongly that the Christian community needs just such a tool, and I wish to help in the only way I am able at this point in time. A catalyst can be a factor in the development of certain breakthroughs in science and medicine. For personal reasons I can only act as a catalyst in this effort, and this is my proposition:

Enclosed you will find a check in the amount of $400.00 (I wish it could be more) to help with publication costs of the booklet. Please do not take what I'm about to say as anything other than a prayerful decision on my part to assure that the contribution will be utilized immediately for the work of our Lord. If by October 1, 1979, the booklet is complete, please send two copies to the P.O. Box listed below. If you have not completed it by then, please send your check returning the contribution. Should uncontrollable circumstances delay its publication, merely drop a note and an extension will be granted. But this money must be used for His work no later than the end of October.

There are many souls being lost daily to the satanical cult of Mormonism. . . . You have no time to lose! . . . Each day that passes without your tool in the hands of the Christian community helps the Mormon influence grow! . . . You have collectively in your minds, the knowledge and power to advance

Christianity . . . to slow down the creeping cancer of a cult. . . . Transfer it from your minds to paper. . . . Teach others to use it. . . . The power of the Word of God has no limits in the hands of the Christian. . . . Do this and your numbers will multiply. . . . More people like myself will see your light in the distance and be drawn to its radiance to help in whatever way they are able.

Even though I can't be with you in body, my mind will reflect on you daily as a group, not yet knowing the potency of their combined talents and gifts. Publish your tool!!! I believe the realization of its influence over many, yet unknown to you, will be beyond your highest expectations.

Remember, Satan is a dangerous foe. . . . His ways are very subtle. . . . Don't allow him to tie you with trivia or worldly pleasures. . . . You have entered the battleground. . . . He is your opponent. . . . Bind him and complete your work. . . . Be the master of this effort. . . . Enter this struggle as though your life depended on it . . . for the lives of many others do!!!!

My prayers will be with you!

A fellow Concerned Christian in spirit.
P.O. Box <u>at later date</u>!
Phoenix, AZ 85001

About halfway through the letter, Jim said, "Whoa! This person means business."

"Who do you suppose this is, Jim?" We examined the envelope and check, turning each over and over.

"I can't imagine who it might be, but he or she is very wise."

"Why do you say that?"

"We not only have a challenge to finish our booklet, but we have financial help and a deadline as well."

JIM AND I TOOK THIS CHALLENGE to Concerned Christians. We collectively took it as a directive from God and got to work. Each of us took a doctrine of the Mormon Church that contrasted with historical Christianity, researched it using LDS scriptures and teachings from their own books, and compared that to the Bible.

I took the responsibility of coordinating and editing the work. Janet took time with me, before she pedaled off to teach swimming at the YMCA each morning, to pray about whatever aspect of the book was before us. I didn't think it would be possible to finish by October 1; but with the line-by-line editing of each member of Concerned Christians, spurred on by the challenge of our wise, anonymous donor, the book was ready to go to press the first of October.

WITH OUR FIRST DRAFT of *Witness to Mormons* tucked neatly into a manila folder and lying on the seat beside me, I drove to D & L Press. The man behind the counter, Bill Pinch, owner of the press, put me at ease immediately with his quiet and unassuming manner.

"Mr. Pinch, our group, Concerned Christians, wants to print about one thousand copies of this manuscript." Then I naïvely inquired, "How much will it cost?"

Bill, gentleman that he is, replied in his soft voice,

"Well, the typesetting alone will be——" He put figures into his hand calculator and showed me an amount that caused me to gulp.

"Mr. Pinch, we only have $400."

Bill looked over the forty-two pages of comparisons, slowly turning over each page, and, without looking up, spoke slowly, "I know one of the authors, and I like what you're trying to do here. I'll make up the difference myself and print it for you."

I was stunned. This man, whom I'd just met, agreed to print our manuscript for less than the cost of the paper!

The booklet has been in print now since 1979, and has sold in over sixty-four countries.

The words of our anonymous benefactor have proved to be prophetic: *"I believe the realization of its [the booklet's] influence over many, yet unknown to you, will be beyond your highest expectations."*

The following is one of countless letters that continue to flow through our office. All testify how God has used this little tool as a catalyst—just as our anonymous donor was for us—to open eyes blinded by the deceiver and turn them toward Christ.

April 9, 1996
To Concerned Christians, Inc.:

I wanted to send you a note today to thank you for the wonderful literature that directly saved me from Mormonism! Even though it was nearly ten years ago that I left the "church," I thank God every day for bringing your book, *Witness to Mormons*, into my life. I know, with no doubt whatsoever, that this volume was

the leading cause for my defection from the Church of
Jesus Christ of Latter-day Saints. It is thoughtfully and
intelligently written and leaves little room for question
as to the theologies of the *Book of Mormon*, Mormonism as a church, and Jesus Christ. It is easily read and
written in an understandable manner. I have read nearly
everything published on the subject of Mormonism over
the past ten years and, truly, this is the best out there!

I am so grateful for your ministry and support you
with my prayers, and, hopefully, soon, my knowledge
and energy as well. I know of your burden for the souls
of those trapped in Mormonism, as well as those potential converts who lack the knowledge to fight the
"logic" of Mormon missionaries. Please let me aid in
the war for souls. I need to do something with all of
this information swimming around in my head!

Thank you again, and God bless you!

Sincerely,

Suzie Ford

We decided to put excerpts of the booklet in weekly
paid ads in the *Mesa Tribune*. Each small block read: DID
YOU KNOW? and followed with one belief of Mormonism
compared to Christianity. These were printed in the fall of
1980 through 1981:

Mormons believe that there is more than one God.[1]

Christians believe that there is only one God. (Deu-
teronomy 4:35; Isaiah 44:6–8; 1 John 5:7; John 10:30.
Please read entire chapter of each book quoted.)

Watch this space each week for more messages.

Concerned Christians

P.O. Box 18, Mesa, AZ 85201

We continued boldly to compare the Mormon god with the God of Christianity for one year:

> The god of Mormonism is flesh and bone vs. the God of Christianity is Spirit.
>
> The god of Mormonism can only be in one place at a time vs. the God of Christianity is omnipresent.
>
> The god of Mormonism is continually progressing vs. the God of Christianity is unchanging.
>
> The christ of Mormonism was begotten by a flesh-and-bone god vs. the Christ of Christianity who was begotten of the Holy Ghost.

Each statement was followed by references for where each teaching was found.

The following year, we invited others to come and speak. We advertised in the *Mesa Tribune*:

> Concerned Christians Is Sponsoring:
>   Dick Baer
>   Director of Ex-Mormons for Jesus of
>   Bakersfield, CA.
>   Dick was born and raised Mormon, married in the Los Angeles temple, graduated from Brigham Young University, and held many leadership positions in the LDS Church, including a stake mission. . . . Our guest will be speaking on "The Most Effective Way to Witness to Mormons" and "The Biblical Test of a Prophet."
>   You are welcome to come and ask questions. We encourage you to "prove all things; hold fast that which is good" (1 Thessalonians 5:21).

I had worked hard on each one of these ads making sure

the facts were straight, the wording non-defensive—just the facts. I prayed after each submission that some open-minded Mormon would read it in the privacy of his or her home and make the decision to reject Mormonism and accept Jesus. It was my constant prayer. Concerned Christians prayed as a group that eyes would be opened. They prayed individually each week, with each new ad, that someone, somewhere, would read and come to know the God of the Bible.

And then, abruptly, the door was slammed shut. September 29, 1982, Max Jennings' editorial read:

Paper Rejects Ad Defaming Mormonism

Most newspapers I know about tend to accept most advertising because in most cases that's the fairest approach. It's also good for business if a newspaper can accept all the ads customers want to pay for.

But this newspaper no longer is going to accept advertising from a group known as Concerned Christians. This organization, composed mostly of former members of the Church of Jesus Christ of Latter-day Saints and some conservative Christians, devotes itself to trying to convince as many people as it can that Mormons are misguided in their beliefs and teachings.

But Mason Dewey's call was the final straw. Dewey, a former Baptist who has been a Mormon convert for twenty-five years, called the *Tribune* to say that the Concerned Christians ad which appeared Saturday was not an ad promoting a faith, but rather an attempt to tear down his own faith.

"Would you print an ad attacking the Jews?" he demanded.

I had a hard time with this question, and asked my boss, publisher Charles Wahlheim, the same question.

Wahlheim turned on his heel, walked into the advertising department, and announced that he didn't want to run any such ads in the future that denigrate a religion. That's his privilege. He's the boss.

The issue was not denying people their freedom of religion at all; it was exposing the secret side of Mormonism. Our desire was that people *could* choose after they knew all the facts.

We would like to have said to Wahlheim, "We know what Judaism teaches. There are no secrets. The Mormon presentation, given to unsuspecting people, is a whitewash. We, as ex-LDS and Concerned Christians, wanted the Mormon hierarchy to come clean and tell its *real* beliefs. Let people decide if they will accept it or not *after* they see all the facts." We exercised our First Amendment rights—freedom of the press. That right was now denied.

Our donor had said, *"You have entered the battleground. . . . Enter this struggle as though your life depended on it . . . for the lives of many others do!!!"* And the struggle was just beginning.

22

Centennial Hall Censure

I T WILL STIR UP a hornet's nest," Jim had said. We expected the uproar from the Mormon hierarchy after the showing of *The Godmakers*. We were willing to take that risk and face the music afterward; but in so doing we prayed eyes would be opened to the truth about Mormonism.

Before the censure of our "DID YOU KNOW?" articles, we secured space in the *Tribune* to advertise the public showing of *The Godmakers*. It would run, the newspaper promised.

Tuesday, March 8, 1983, Concerned Christians showed—not behind anyone's back and in the largest facility we could find—the film *The Godmakers*. Centennial Hall was packed with approximately 1,500 people.

Jim and I were among many ex-Mormons who were interviewed in this documentary. The film was shown by Ex-Mormons for Jesus throughout the United States. Little did we know it would light a fuse for an explosion. The aftershocks among the religious in our community still rumble, years later.

The secret doors of Mormonism, long held shut to the public, were opened wide for all to see. All was unveiled. The wolf was caught half-dressed in his sheepskin.

The film defined altars. It exposed the flesh-and-bone god of Mormonism and made clear this was not the biblical Jesus. He was only one of "Heavenly Father's" spirit children along with Lucifer.

Those of us who were ex-Mormons had worshiped at both altars. We knew the difference.

We hoped to stop the lemming-like march of obedience to false prophets, but the roar that followed almost blew us away.

As Goliath defied and mocked the armies of Israel and Israel's God, so our ranks were challenged—the line drawn in the sand.

Wednesday, March 9, 1983, the *Mesa Tribune* editorial by Max Jennings read:

Group Stones Mormons
in the Name of Christianity

A lynch mob gathered in Centennial Hall Tuesday night. It was your garden variety lynch mob, I suppose, people who know what they want before they show up.

This time, in the best tradition of religious freedom in this country, the mobsters were out to disembowel a particular faith.

Religion, of course, is a theme that can pit brother against brother, nation against nation, and man against himself. In fact, many great wars in history have been fought in the name of religion.

While we hoped some would see truth and accept it, the words that hurt most were from other religious people. Max was one. He went on to say in his lengthy article:

> If what I saw Tuesday night is love, I must have had the wrong Sunday school lessons back in that dusty west Texas Methodist Church of my childhood.

But those who knew us, and many who didn't, called and sent letters supporting our position. Our pastor titled his sermon the following Sunday, "You Can't Keep People From Shouting About the Lord." He picked us up out of the sand, and we dusted ourselves off, ready for the next wave. His text included Luke 19:39–40:

> "Some of the Pharisees in the crowd said to Jesus, 'Teacher, rebuke your disciples!'
> 'I tell you,' he replied, 'if they keep quiet, the stones will cry out.' "
> Jesus knew the heart of man.
> You can't keep people from shouting about the Lord.

Prefacing his remarks with his reluctance to do so, our pastor reminded his congregation:

> My charge as a preacher is to proclaim the good news of Jesus Christ, not the bad news of any heresy. . . . Today I must speak up, however, because of the current controversy sparked by the showing of the film *The Godmakers* at Centennial Hall and the editorial

the following morning by the *Mesa Tribune*'s Max Jennings.

Americans believe that open, earnest research is helpful in the sciences, in government, in all branches of knowledge. Should religion be the only dimension of reality to be unprobed? Or if researched, should the findings be censored?

Each point he made affirmed our reasons for showing the film. He went on to say:

Frankly, I am afraid of Jennings' stance. In the name of community tranquility, the South tolerated the Ku Klux Klan. In the name of tolerance, the churches of Germany held their peace when they should have been lashing out at Hitlerism. In more recent days the Disciples of Christ have been under attack for tolerating the vagaries of Jim Jones, who finally led his tortured disciples to their gruesome end.

What would Jennings have us do when we disagree and think our antagonists are in danger? Would Jennings also have us say nothing about the teachings of the Reverend Moon, of the Hare Krishnas, or the Children of God, or anyone else? If we disagree, must we keep quiet?

Dr. Lawson ended his sermon with six truths we stand on as a church. This was the last one:

We have only one Lord and we have only one Book. We adhere to the authority of the Scriptures called the Bible. We do not believe it has been replaced by later revelations any more than we believe Jesus Christ has been made a back number by some latter-day prophet. These things we must say. We cannot be silent any more than Jesus' early disciples could be gagged on the day of his triumphal entry into Jerusalem. You can't keep people from shouting about the Lord.

The congregation stood and clapped at the end. I'll never forget the overwhelming comfort from God I felt in church that day. The God of all comfort reached down through His people, gathered up our shattered emotions, and replaced them with His unfathomable love.

THE COMMUNITY, in quite a stir, generated letters to the editor like Ping-Pong balls. First, a letter from a Mormon, and then from a Christian. Each morning's news brought either a relieved sigh as one would support or an "ouch" when a critic would take a potshot.

Brother, the Soul Is at Stake

It's very true that we all have a right to choose, but unless you have the facts, choosing can be difficult.

The Concerned Christians may seem to Jennings to attack Mormons, but what they say, they say in public. The Mormons, on the other hand . . .

The Bible teaches of false prophets. . . . Our children are prey. . . . Who more than ex-Mormons who have "paid the price" should tell the truth about the Mormon beliefs? . . .

Give the people the facts; they can make a choice.

I appreciate Jennings' admitting that his words

(*attack* and *hate*) were not their words. As it appears, he attacks men and women who sacrifice a great deal to warn people of danger.

—*Mary Wiedenhaupt*

Be Grateful for Good Neighbors

I am grateful for Max Jennings' column on religious hatred and intolerance.

Fifty-six years ago I was brought to Arizona by my parents, and in school, for the first time, I met my Mormon neighbors. It was not mine to argue with their tenets but it was mine then and now to be grateful for good neighbors. . . .

Bitterness and hatred and intolerance were very much present in another village centuries ago, and they raised a cross against the sky.

Mesa is still a great city and cannot afford to clasp intolerance and hatred to its breast—it must be concerned, about love and about tomorrow.

—*Rev. Msgr. Robert J. Donohoe,*
Ecumenical Officer,
Roman Catholic Diocese of Phoenix

I Know the Church Is True

I would like to express my gratitude to Max Jennings and to thank those he represents. . . .

I am a Mormon and I know the church is true. I have not been brain-washed, as the Concerned Christians would have one believe, but rather, I was a convert, and I was converted after much fasting and praying.

I hope he does not have a negative view of the Mormons after what he has been taught. Yes, the doctrine is confusing if you dive into the meat of it, but if you take it step by step, inch by inch, precept upon precept, and line upon line, you will find, as I did, the gospel is true.

—*Robert Graham, Mesa*

And then the publisher of the newspaper scored points with this slam:

Sunday, March 13, 1983. OPINION EDITORIALS:

Freedom for All Faiths

Since an organization known as Concerned Christians showed a propaganda film about the Mormon Church Tuesday night, a lot of heartening things have occurred in this community.

Jews, Catholics, and Methodists, and representatives of a dozen other faiths have expressed outrage in the attack on the Church of Jesus Christ of Latter-day Saints . . .

Attacks on religious beliefs will not be allowed in advertising if we can prevent them.

At the same time—our disgust unequivocally stated at the religious attack of Tuesday night—we feel it's equally important to allow the Concerned Christians organization its forum.

This organization has the right to rent Centennial Hall, the right of free speech, and the right to pursue its own religious beliefs and practices.

There are some in recent days so outraged by the Tuesday night affair they seem to have lost sight of this principle.

This aside, the Tuesday night attack on the Mormons is repugnant to the majority in this community. We think rather than divide this community, however, it may have the effect of reuniting us anew so Mesa will continue to be one of the best places to live in this nation.

—*Charles A. Wahlheim,*
Publisher

Though it seemed, at times, we were losing the battle, many read and considered. Some possibly examined, for the first time, the foundations of their faith.

The controversy and subsequent uproar was worth it all if only one soul was saved. Our Concerned Christians Fall 1983 Newsletter told of far different "news" that caused the angels in heaven to rejoice:

God is so good, and the hard work is really beginning to produce Christian fruit. There are so many things to tell you about. For example, in one week's time we saw the following: On Friday, a doctor made his decision for the Lord.

On Sunday in Prescott, AZ, an 83-year-old man stood up during the question-and-answer time and said he was a lifelong Mormon, a high priest, and for the last 17 years, a temple worker at the temple in Mesa. He said he wanted everybody in the audience to know that what had been taught that night in the film *The Godmakers* and by Jim was absolutely true. Then said he wanted to know how to write his letter of resignation.

On Monday, a 30-year-old woman with two children, born in the LDS Church, called at the recommendation of a policeman, and said she needed to talk to someone. She was scared and in tears, but finally agreed to meet with Jim that night. From 8:00 P.M. to 1:00 A.M., he and Judy shared the Scriptures with her. She renounced Mormonism and accepted Christ. She kept saying over and over again that it was such a relief to know that God had forgiven and forgotten her sins. (She had been told by her bishop that one more "sin" would finalize her condemnation.)

On Tuesday, a woman, whose son is a bishop . . . made her commitment to the Lord.

Wednesday, a 16-year-old Mormon came to the Lord in our office.

Thursday morning, a 35-year-old Mormon man came to the office and viewed the films. When they were finished, he and Jim discussed the difference between Mormon and Christian doctrines. After two-and-one-half hours he accepted Christ.

That evening, a man brought his 35-year-old Mormon girlfriend over, and she made her decision for Christ.

On Friday, a woman and her daughter came to the office and admitted that Mormonism was wrong and they both wanted to make their confession of faith in the Lord.

On Saturday, a young married couple (the husband, a Christian, and the wife, a Mormon) came to the office. She made her decision for Christ that night.

During that week, we got a letter with more good

news. Jim had been asked to come to a home where some LDS missionaries were to be teaching. When an attempt was made to get them to respond to questions about testing their prophet, the senior companion missionary refused to answer and said he didn't think it was important. The junior companion watched all this and acknowledged it wasn't right. The next week he called the couple and has met with them on a couple of occasions, now to discuss the Bible. He said he was amazed that the gospel of Christ was so simple. Keep all these people in your prayers.

Perhaps we were naïve in our zeal and fierce desire to allow the public to see the hidden and blasphemous doctrine of the LDS Church. But maybe God used our naïveté and determination to expose the doctrine of demons and protect hundreds from innocently becoming a part of this heresy. Perhaps this was a window of opportunity that will never be opened again.

Yes, Max Jennings' words hurt and cut to the core of my weakest area of self-esteem and emotions. Who wants to be known as one who "throws stones" or is part of a "lynch mob"? However, if I tell the truth publicly, I'd better not plan to win a popularity contest. As even Max would say: Criticism comes with the territory.

Today, I encourage others to be the best friend they can be to Mormons—to open their homes and lives to them and to love them. As Jim says, "Let the light of Christ show through you."

I'm glad I participated in this effort to expose the heresy of Mormonism. It was costly in terms of hurt feelings and misunderstandings. But somehow, I believe Jesus would have done the same thing when I remember how He chased the money changers out of the temple in Jerusalem. He said, "It is written . . . 'My house will be called a house of prayer,' but you are making it a 'den of robbers' " (Matthew 21:13). The Mormon temple is a den of robbers, stealing the souls of innocent victims.

Today, twenty-eight years since leaving the Mormon Church, I am still saying, "Don't you see the LDS 'gospel' is a perversion of the gospel of Jesus Christ? Get out! Get out, before it's too late!"

Jesus never condemned a person for zeal, only for lack of it:

> These are the words of the Amen, the faithful and true witness, the ruler of God's creation. I know your deeds, that you are neither cold nor hot. I wish you were either one or the other! So, because you are luke-warm—neither hot nor cold—I am about to spit you out of my mouth. (Revelation 3:14–16)

Our zeal, however, was not without cost and consequences. But, like the pearl of great price Jesus spoke of in Matthew 13:44–46, it was worth everything: even, as we were about to discover, success in the business world.

23

The Choice

THERE COMES A TIME in every life when we approach a fork in the road. We must decide to go right or left. And with the choosing, we know there will be no turning back. For Jim and me, that choice was easy.

Jim dropped his car keys on the kitchen counter. "I was called into the executive vice president's office today."

"For?"

"A little warning, I suppose you could say."

"Really? What kind?" I turned off the dishwasher to hear every word.

"John said several Mormon, big-money depositors are making noises about my speaking out on Mormonism."

"What are they saying?"

"They're saying the bank better shut me up or else they'll pull out their money."

"What did you tell him, Jim?"

"You know what I said. I told him I feel the Lord has

called me to do this and I have to continue. John asked me to at least tone it down a bit."

Jim and I had discussed needing someone to carry out the many speaking engagements on a permanent basis. Every weekend for months ahead was filled with teaching sessions at churches from every denomination. The ministry kept growing and took more time as the weeks and months went by.

"Even if the Mormon depositors continue badgering my bosses," Jim vowed, "I cannot stop speaking out about Mormonism—no matter what."

FOUR MONTHS LATER, Jim received a memo to come into the executive office again. The Mormon depositors continued pressuring the bank. Jim was taken off his job as assistant vice president over personnel and given a temporary community-service assignment.

After the job was finished, the bank offered Jim a branch manager's job. He refused, saying he preferred working in personnel.

One last time, Jim met with John in the senior officer's suite. "Jim"—John's voice ached with compassion—"you must make a choice. Either stop speaking out about the Mormon religion or we will have to let you go."

"Well, I guess I'll be leaving, John." Jim couldn't believe how calm he felt.

So, on this warm day in June 1983, after eleven years with the bank, Jim walked away from the glass skyscraper in downtown Phoenix. "What have I done?" he mumbled to himself. "How are Judy and I going to make ends meet?"

I T HAPPENED." Jim walked in the back door.

"What?" I didn't expect Jim home from work so soon.

"Today I made the choice."

"Am I going to have to pull it out of you? What?"

"It's going to be Concerned Christians now, full time."

"I knew this would happen, Jim. I knew you'd be doing this full time one day."

"I just didn't think it would be me." Jim frowned and slumped onto a kitchen chair. "Personnel was my life. I enjoy everything about it—the social and business contacts, dealing with big businesses. It's what I do best."

I listened as Jim pushed his car keys around on the table. "But, God traded my personnel job for Concerned Christians, didn't He?" He looked at me and I smiled.

"He sure did, and I'm glad. I believe this is what He had planned all along."

G OD WANTED US TO EXPOSE, by His light, the secrets done in darkness. With regular speaking engagements and a number of churches and individuals supporting Concerned Christians, the board decided to give Jim a salary. We had our marching orders:

> Have nothing to do with the fruitless deeds of darkness, but rather expose them. For it is shameful even to mention what the disobedient do in secret. But every-

thing exposed by the light becomes visible, for it is light that makes everything visible. (Ephesians 5:11–14)

With our orders came plenty of resistance. Threatening calls came from nameless people in the dead of night. Some only left one word, "Bigot"; others a sentence, "You're of the devil"; and then they'd hang up. For a peace-loving person like me, these words stung—leaving their sickening venom.

It seemed to me God chose the most unlikely person for such a ministry. I shy away from confrontation in any form. *How did this happen? God, do you suppose maybe you can find somebody else to do this? Are you sure this is what you want us to do?*

To answer my pleading, God sent a constant flow of people to our home and to our support-group meetings who needed our help. An inner joy sprang up in me as each found hope in Christ and accepted His death on the cross as payment for their sins, rather than trying to earn salvation by good works.

Jim found completeness in his new job. "All my experience in my job with the bank prepared me for this. Besides, there's great reward in my Concerned Christians work. It replaces everything I enjoyed as a personnel director."

J IM AND I WANDERED OFF THE PATH of historical Christianity in 1967 because Jesus was not the center of our lives. We had lacked a burning love for Him, and it was easy to be drawn into false teachings. We simply hadn't known whom we professed to follow. Jesus said in Revelation 2:4, "You have forsaken your first love." And so we had.

I didn't know, when I first came to Arizona with Jim on a business trip, I would eventually realize that the "finest people you'll ever meet" were the most deceived. I hadn't a clue I'd someday be reaching out to them, offering the real joy found only in Jesus, hoping they'd see their efficient organization had left them without peace or hope.

"How can such good people be wrong?" I had asked when Jim first introduced me to his Mormon business associates. It took living the life of those "good people" to find the answer.

I didn't know then that Satan actively lies to good people, offering them luscious-looking fruit. It's the same fruit Satan offered Adam and Eve—to be like God. The ultimate goal of Mormonism is to be good enough to become a god of your own planet. Adam and Eve were banished from God's presence for believing Satan's lie.

> Do not love the world or anything in the world. If anyone loves the world, the love of the Father is not in him. For everything in the world—the cravings of sinful man, the lust of his eyes and the boasting of what he has and does—comes not from the Father but from the world. (1 John 2:15–16)

I did not know God's Word then—today, I do. It is my prayer that the good people in the Mormon Church will see clearly the lie they have accepted, turn from their false religion that deceived them, and follow Jesus only—the One who is the Way, the Truth, and the Life.

I know God now in a way that perhaps I wouldn't have if I hadn't taken this detour from my Christian roots. God allowed me to wander through a dark and lonely path of my own choosing. All the while, He held out to me the sunshine of His love, waiting for me to turn from that dark path to a close walk with Him.

I know He is Immanuel—God with us—and He will never leave me nor forsake me. He has proven that time and again in whatever circumstance I have found myself.

Getting to know God for who He is, not a god who is far away and distant from the daily affairs of my life, has been worth everything. My life has meaning and purpose. It is satisfying and rewarding. And I don't need to wear myself out trying to meet the arbitrary goals set forth by men in an effort to please a god who is no god at all.

A steady stream of searching people comes to our in-home office. Young adults come to find ways to witness to their Mormon friends and relatives, many times bringing them along to hear truth about the real teachings of Mormonism.

Parents come for counsel on how to deal with a son who secretly joined the Mormon Church and is now on a mission for the LDS Church in a foreign country. Estranged husbands and wives come for support because their spouse was counseled to divorce them and choose a strong LDS spouse instead.

Jim and I begin our day in prayer for each other and for the ones who are still in darkness. Our lives bubble over with joy from knowing God alone—the one true God, who gives wisdom and knowledge and every good thing we have on this earth. We know that:

> The true worshipers will worship the Father in spirit and truth, for they are the kind of worshipers the Father seeks. God is spirit, and his worshipers must worship in spirit and in truth. (John 4:23b–24)

It is our desire to let Christ's light tear down and disarm the deeds done in darkness, to disrobe the wolf in sheep's clothing that devours so many innocent victims.

I have no regrets, for my faithful God redeemed me— His weak one—and brought me to an understanding of His grace, reminding me that this is all I need. I am surrounded by His unfathomable love. I long for others to know the depths of His love, too.

"Being confident of this, that He who began a good work in [me] will carry it on to completion until the day of Christ Jesus" (Philippians 1:6).

Epilogue

IN AUGUST 1986 Concerned Christians and Ex-Mormons for Jesus met in Salt Lake City, Utah, where we were told of the heavy influence of Mormonism in the South Pacific Islands. Jim and I prayed about what we could do to help—thinking in terms of sending literature. But God's plans for us were far different from what we expected. We both sensed Him tugging at our hearts, saying, "I don't want you to send literature, I want *you* to go." And go we did.

From June 1987 to August 1993, Jim and I traveled among the Samoan and Tongan islands in the South Pacific. We taught in theological colleges and churches of every denomination about Mormonism.

We heard over and over, "We have been praying for someone to help us know about Mormonism, because many of our people leave our churches to become Mormon."

While still living in the Islands, we joined hands with South Seas Christian Ministries to bring Bible camps and seminars for pastors and layleaders throughout the South

Pacific each summer. This ministry also has provided food, clothing, and portable sawmills after devastating hurricanes, while providing spiritual nourishment for the traditional churches.

After moving back to the States, Jim and I continued to work with SSCM each summer from 1994–2000, taking teams of resource people to the Islands.

The need for teaching about Mormonism continues, as well as the opportunity for growth and equipping God's people in the South Pacific countries.

The spring of 2001 ushered in a new era for Concerned Christians. Needing office space outside our home, a building on an acre of property became available two blocks behind the Mesa LDS temple. This facility adequately provides for our expanding ministry with room for growth.

Supporters are giving generously, donating office equipment, time, and funds for the ongoing of Concerned Christians.

Only God knows where the future will lead.

As our anonymous donor wrote so many years ago: "All great achievements are the results of humble beginnings, combined with perseverance and guided by the Word of God." Concerned Christians is still relentlessly pursuing God's children who have been spiritually blinded by Mormonism.

The Lord has called many others to join in this pursuit. Together, we will continue holding out the Word of truth boldly, and drawing the deceived into the loving arms of Jesus.

Resources

The Road to Mormonism Beckons Travelers Unawares

Unaware of the Bible

> For you have been born again, not of perishable seed, but of imperishable, through the living and enduring word of God. (1 Peter 1:23)

Many Christians believe the Bible to be God's infallible Word. The problem is not knowing what it says. Jim and I were among those who believed in, but were not students of, the Bible. Both of us had heard many sermons growing up and were regular Sunday school attendees, but we had never studied the Bible for ourselves.

Paul describes in 2 Corinthians 11:3–4 (KJV) *exactly* what happened to Jim and me:

> But I fear, lest by any means, as the serpent beguiled Eve through his subtlety, so your minds should

be corrupted from the simplicity that is in Christ. For if he that cometh preacheth another Jesus, whom we have not preached, or if ye receive another spirit, which ye have not received, or another gospel, which ye have not accepted, ye might well bear with him.

The Bible is the Christian's road map. On our journey with Jesus, it's our responsibility to study His directions for us in His Word. Jim and I left the path of historic Christianity and followed three paths that led us astray.

The path to another Jesus

The Jesus taught by Mormon prophets has no saving power:

Joseph Smith taught that there were certain sins so grievous that man may commit, that they will place the transgressors beyond the power of the atonement of Christ.[1]

If the Mormon would be saved, he must shed his own blood. The Mormon Jesus is the spirit-brother of Lucifer and is only one of many gods who are continually progressing.[2]

> For the message of the cross is foolishness to those who are perishing, but to us who are being saved it is the power of God. (1 Corinthians 1:18)

An old hymn says, "There is power, power, wonder-working power, in the precious blood of the Lamb." And, indeed, the redemptive power in the shed blood of Jesus is all we need for salvation. Our own blood would do nothing but stain the carpet.

But God chose the foolish things of the world to

shame the wise; God chose the weak things of the world to shame the strong. He chose the lowly things of this world and the despised things—and the things that are not—to nullify the things that are, so that no one may boast before him. It is because of him that you are in Christ Jesus, who has become for us wisdom from God—that is, our righteousness, holiness and redemption. Therefore, as it is written: "Let him who boasts boast in the Lord" (1 Corinthians 1:27–31).

The path to another spirit

In the Mormon Church, we were baptized by one who had the authority to do so, they said. Baptism performed in non-Mormon churches is not valid, since they do not have this authority (according to Mormon teaching). Before immersing us, these words were stated: "By the power and authority of the holy Melchizedek priesthood, which I hold, I baptize you in the name of the Father and the Son and the Holy Ghost." And afterward we received the "gift of the Holy Ghost" by the laying on of hands of those having the authority.[3]

Did the men who baptized us into the Mormon Church truly have the power and authority of the Melchizedek priesthood? First John 4:1 teaches us to test the spirits to see whether they are from God.

Hebrews 7:11–28 clearly shows Jesus as the permanent and only one who holds the Melchizedek priesthood. Verse 24 reads, "But this man, because he continueth ever, hath an unchangeable priesthood" (KJV).

In our King James Bible—the only version accepted by Latter-day Saints—a reference (the number 5) by the words "an unchangeable priesthood" gives this further explanation: "Or, which passeth not from one to another." The Mormon priesthood is passed from one priesthood bearer to another by the laying on of hands (see *Priesthood* in the Glossary of Mormon Terms).

By claiming to hold this priesthood, Mormons are placing themselves on the same rank as Jesus. Jesus warned us, saying,

> For many will come in my name, claiming, "I am the Christ," and will deceive many. (Matthew 24:5)

Clearly, we were deceived and accepted "another spirit."

The path to another gospel

Galatians 1:6–9 tells us there is no other gospel:

> I am astonished that you are so quickly deserting the one who called you by the grace of Christ and are turning to a different gospel—which is really no gospel at all. Evidently some people are throwing you into confusion and are trying to pervert the gospel of Christ. But even if we or an angel from heaven should preach a gospel other than the one we preached to you, let him be eternally condemned! As we have already said, so now I say again: If anybody is preaching to you a gospel other than what you accepted, let him be eternally condemned!

The angel Moroni, we were told, brought the *Book of Mormon* on golden plates to Joseph Smith. Joseph preached that Jesus and God, two distinct personages, told him all other sects—Methodist, Baptist, Presbyterian, and all other denominations—were wrong and that he would be the bearer of a new or "restored" gospel, thus bringing to the world the only true church. Proverbs 30:5–6 gives us a warning:

> Every word of God is flawless; he is a shield to those who take refuge in him. Do not add to his words, or he will rebuke you and prove you a liar.

We did all these things because we did not know God's Word, nor did we have an active relationship with Jesus. If we had, we would have questioned this new and different teaching.

And in Acts 17:11 we see the Bereans were commended for searching the Scriptures to see if Paul's teaching lined up with what they already knew:

> Now the Bereans were of more noble character than the Thessalonians, for they received the message with great eagerness and examined the Scriptures every day to see if what Paul said was true.

Walter Martin, in his book *The Kingdom of the Cults*, says,

> The American Banking Association . . . sends hundreds of bank tellers to Washington in order to teach them to detect counterfeit money, which is a great source of a loss of revenue to the Treasury Department. It is most interesting that during the entire two-week training program, no teller touches counterfeit money.

Only the original passes through his hands. The reason for this is that the American Banking Association is convinced that if a man is thoroughly familiar with the original he will not be deceived by the counterfeit bill, no matter how much like the original it appears. It is the contention of this writer that if the average Christian would become familiar once again with the great foundations of his faith, he would be able to detect those counterfeit elements so apparent in the cult systems, which set them apart from biblical Christianity.[4]

Unaware of Cults

The marks of a cult are these:

1. *A man or woman who has proclaimed himself/herself as ultimate authority.*

Every cult, historically, is led by a charismatic personality who is able to persuade people. Joseph Smith swayed many people by his proclamations—and convinced even his own wife, Emma, that God had told him through a revelation to have more wives; she would be damned if she didn't obey this law:

> And I command mine handmaid, Emma Smith, to abide and cleave unto my servant Joseph, and to none else. But if she will not abide this commandment she shall be destroyed, saith the Lord; for I am the Lord thy God, and will destroy her if she abide not in my law (*Doctrine and Covenants*, 132:54).[5]

We should question, when we consider a person's integrity, who gets the glory. Lucifer said, "I will make myself like the Most High" (Isaiah 14:14). He was cast out of heaven and into "the depths of the pit" (v. 15). Jesus said we should call no man rabbi or leader, master or father:

> Nor are you to be called "teacher," for you have one Teacher, the Christ. The greatest among you will be your servant. For whoever exalts himself will be humbled, and whoever humbles himself will be exalted. (Matthew 23:10–12)

Terrible consequences occur when a person glorifies himself instead of God. On May 26, 1844, Joseph Smith claimed he was greater than Jesus:

> I have more to boast of than ever any man had. I am the only man that has ever been able to keep a whole church together since the days of Adam. A large majority of the whole have stood by me. Neither Paul, John, Peter, nor Jesus ever did it. I boast that no man ever did such a work as I. The followers of Jesus ran away from Him: but the Latter-day Saints never ran away from me yet.[6]

Joseph Smith died one month later, on June 27, 1844, after making this boast.

2. *Additional books that are considered Scripture.*

Joseph Smith claimed he was given golden plates that contained what was later called the *Book of Mormon*. In addition, the *Doctrine and Covenants*, which contains revelations given to Joseph, and the *Pearl of Great Price*—all are considered Scripture by Latter-day Saints.

Many cults promote the false idea that God has revealed

something special to them. This is usually truth that supposedly has never before been revealed and supersedes and contradicts all previous revelations. Sun Myung Moon's claim is that the mission of Christ was left unfinished and the world is now ready for the completion of Christ's work on earth.[7]

In the *Book of Mormon*, the writer attempts to validate its importance by saying, "Woe be unto him that shall say: We have received the word of God, and we need not more of God, for we have enough!" (*Book of Mormon*, 2 Nephi 28:29).

Joseph Smith said, "I told the Brethren that the Book of Mormon was the most correct book on earth."[8]

3. *Redefine God and Jesus* (see p. 168, *The Path to Another Jesus*. Jesus is redefined by Joseph Smith).

The most important question we can ask about another's belief is: Who is Christ to you? This is the question Jesus asked His disciples:

> Once when Jesus was praying in private and his disciples were with Him, he asked them, "Who do the crowds say I am?"
>
> They replied, "Some say John the Baptist; others say Elijah; and still others, that one of the prophets of long ago has come back to life."
>
> "But what about you?" he asked. "Who do you say I am?"
>
> Peter answered, "The Christ of God" (Luke 9:18–20).

Mormon leaders teach that Jesus is merely the spirit-brother of Lucifer,[9] the firstborn of all the spirit children of Father.[10]

Who is Jesus to us? This is the most important question we can ask ourselves. The key is in John 1: "In the beginning was the Word, and the Word was with God, and the Word was God. He was with God in the beginning" (vv. 1–2).

> Yet to all who received him, to those who believed in his name, he gave the right to become children of God—children born not of natural descent, nor of human decision or a husband's will, but born of God. The Word became flesh and made his dwelling among us. We have seen his glory, the glory of the One and Only, who came from the Father, full of grace and truth. (vv. 12–14)

In the Mormon scripture we find who or what is really the important power in Mormonism:

> And without the ordinances thereof, and the authority of the priesthood, the power of godliness is not manifest unto men in the flesh. (*Doctrine and Covenants*, 84:21)
> And also all they who receive this priesthood receive me, saith the Lord. (*Doctrine and Covenants*, 84:35)

No matter what the particular beliefs of any cult may be, the one common denominator they all possess is a denial of the biblical teaching on the deity of Jesus Christ.[11]

Jim and I were uninformed concerning the cults. When we were taught by the Mormon missionaries that Joseph Smith claimed God *and* Jesus appeared to him—two separate beings—*that* should have been a red flag for us.

In retrospect, we see how we were prime candidates for deception, because we only had a secondhand knowledge of God's Word and no knowledge of the cults.

Unaware of Satan

We don't usually go out searching to do something wrong. But "your enemy the devil prowls around like a roaring lion looking for someone to devour" (1 Peter 5:8). Satan's turf is this earth.

Those of us who have fallen prey to cults are generally nominal Christians who want to do what is right, but are uninformed as to Satan's subtle ways.

Second Corinthians 11:13–15 describes our enemy:

> For such men are false apostles, deceitful workmen, masquerading as apostles of Christ. And no wonder, for Satan himself masquerades as an angel of light. It is not surprising, then, if his servants masquerade as servants of righteousness. Their end will be what their actions deserve.

We are in a battle here on planet Earth. Most of us are simply unaware of it. Ephesians 6:10–18 tells us how to arm ourselves:

> Finally, be strong in the Lord and in his mighty power. Put on the full armor of God so that you can take your stand against the devil's schemes. For our struggle is not against flesh and blood, but against the rulers, against the authorities, against the powers of this

dark world and against the spiritual forces of evil in the heavenly realms. Therefore put on the full armor of God, so that when the day of evil comes, you may be able to stand your ground.

Jim and I were totally unarmed—vulnerable to the fierce battle going on for our souls. Hoodwinked, we swallowed the bait of an "angel of light"—hook, line, and sinker. We never talked about Satan. Frankly, I never even thought about his existence. What I found is, as in any battle, if you don't know your enemy, then you're likely to be overcome by him.

Satan is alive and well. But those who are in Christ Jesus have a defender who is strong. "Because the one who is in you is greater than the one who is in the world" (1 John 4:4).

Jesus said to His disciples on the night before His crucifixion, "Pray that you will not fall into temptation" (Luke 22:40). How seriously we should take Jesus' admonition. But we, like Jesus' disciples, are prone to fall asleep.

Jim and I didn't know our Lord well enough to distinguish Him from a false Christ. We didn't know His Word well enough to distinguish it from a false gospel. We didn't test the spirits and so accepted a false one. We depended on outward appearances and were swayed by emotionalism, and yet Jeremiah 17:9 warns, "The heart is deceitful above all things and beyond cure."

The Mormon missionaries teach a prospective follower to pray until he receives the "burning in the bosom." It all seems so innocent.

"There is a way that seems right to a man, but in the end it leads to death" (Proverbs 14:12).

The Road Out of Mormonism Is Paved With Perseverance

Persevere in Letting Go

> What fellowship can light have with darkness? . . . "Therefore come out from them and be separate, says the Lord" (2 Corinthians 6:14–17).

Hanging onto the trappings of Mormonism prolongs the agony. A healthy step is to let go of the past and go forward. Paul says in Philippians 3:13b:

> Forgetting what is behind and straining toward what is ahead, I press on toward the goal to win the prize for which God has called me heavenward in Christ Jesus.

Many who have a sincere desire to leave the LDS Church fail to take this step right away and cause themselves further hurt.

Letting go of Mormonism was a priority for our family.

It symbolized turning away from false teachings and looking heavenward. Chapter 16 tells about the burning of all our Mormon paraphernalia—our books, our garments, family preparedness charts, etc. I sold some food-storage items (see chapter 18) and discarded all the rest.

Many have told of the great load lifted from their shoulders after relinquishing the above and acknowledging the following:

1. Acknowledge Joseph Smith as a false prophet and those succeeding him as false prophets.[1]

2. Acknowledge that Mormon scriptures contradict the Bible and cause confusion.[2]

3. Acknowledge the Latter-day Saints Church as a false religion as compared to historical Christianity.[3]

Persevere in Finding a Bible-based Church

We needed time together as a family (chapter 17) to get in touch with each other again and to focus on what we wanted to achieve as a family. We needed an unhurried time in the wilderness—Usery Pass Park—to search out God's will for our lives. We also needed other mature Christians for encouragement and example. It is important to seek fellowship in the body of Christ. We prayed as a family for God to guide us to a church that pleased Him; we didn't want to be led astray again.

A life reformed, but lacking spiritual direction, is open to other false religions, as Jesus taught in Matthew 12:43–45:

> When an evil spirit comes out of a man, it goes

through arid places seeking rest and does not find it. Then it says, "I will return to the house I left." When it arrives, it finds the house unoccupied, swept clean and put in order. Then it goes and takes with it seven other spirits more wicked than itself, and they go in and live there. And the final condition of that man is worse than the first.

Don't jump into just any church. Wait for God's guidance. But don't put this off. The sooner you find your church family, the sooner the healing will begin.

Persevere in a Bible Reading Program

The Bible became brand-new to us because we looked at it trying to discern God's will, not trying to make it fit Mormon doctrine. It's important to have a good study Bible. The King James is only one of many versions. Newer translations make studying easier (see chapter 18).

I began by reading the King James alongside *The Living Bible*, a paraphrased version, until I was able to let go of the King James. It's amazing how many habits are entrenched and hard to change. The Mormon Church only accepts the King James Version of the Bible and teaches that it is the only reliable translation. Today, I use the *New International Version*.

The important thing is to put on the full armor of God as Ephesians 6:10–18 tells us (see chapter 20).

Your pastor may recommend a devotional or Bible study method. A trip to your local Christian bookstore will be enlightening. There are many daily devotionals available. Some include:

Our Daily Bread, RBC Ministries, Grand Rapids, MI 49555–0001.

The Upper Room, Daily Devotional Guide, P.O. Box 10926, Des Moines, IA 50347–0926.

My Utmost for His Highest by Oswald Chambers.

The important thing is to study God's Word daily.

Persevere in Removing Your Name From LDS Membership Rolls

Even though it took two years for our names to be removed from LDS Church records, it now can be done in a much more efficient way. Some suggestions are as follows:

Address your letter to:

President Gordon B. Hinckly

(or current Mormon president)

50 East North Temple

Salt Lake City, UT 84150

Send copies of this letter to your last known bishop and stake president or, if not known, to your last known ward or town where you were last active in the church. Send all three letters by certified mail.

Include these six points in your letter:

1. State that you are asking that your name(s) be removed from the records of the LDS Church.

2. State your testimony that Joseph Smith is a false prophet and that the Mormon Church is not Christian. Elaborate as much as you'd like, using the Scriptures from the

Bible that pointed you in the right direction.

3. Make a strong statement for Jesus Christ being the Lord of your life and the Bible being the *only* Word of God.

4. State that you have no intentions of attending a bishop's court, because you are not guilty of anything and you no longer recognize them as having any authority over you.

5. State that their return letter is not to contain any mention of ex-communication because this is your decision and not theirs.

6. State that you expect them to observe your right to privacy and not to send anyone, write, or call in an attempt to change your mind. Let them know you are aware of what they believe are the eternal consequences of your decision. Let them know your decision is firm.

If you have any questions concerning removal of your name from LDS Church records, write:

Concerned Christians
P.O. Box 18
Mesa, AZ 85211

The Road to Eternal Life Is Through Jesus Christ

The Detour

Adam and Eve took the wrong path, detouring the course for all mankind.

Adam and Eve disobeyed God's law in the Garden of Eden, ending their special communion with Him and bringing about spiritual death. Mormon doctrine teaches that Adam and Eve's disobedience in the Garden was good. They say it had to happen so that man could procreate (see chapter 9). However, this was the very act that caused all mankind to inherit the sin nature.

In distorting this event—calling bad "good"—Mormons have missed the whole point of why we need Jesus. This one sin caused all mankind to fall and changed our relationship, or fellowship, with God.

The Way

Because mankind detoured, God provided the gate—Jesus Christ—through whom we reach eternal life.

It's only when we receive Christ as our only hope, the sacrifice or ransom for our sin—our rebellion against God or sin nature—that we inherit eternal life. God provided only one way for us to receive eternal life with Him, and it is through and in Jesus' blood shed on the cross:

> Therefore, there is now no condemnation for those who are in Christ Jesus, because through Christ Jesus the law of the Spirit of life set me free from the law of sin and death. For what the law was powerless to do in that it was weakened by the sinful nature, God did by sending his own Son in the likeness of sinful man to be a sin offering. (Romans 8:1–3)

The Cross

Mormons are taught that the cross is an evil sign. Let's look at what the cross means. In the Old Testament, Numbers 21:4–9, the children of Israel wanted something more—as Eve did in the Garden—to eat. God had provided all they needed in the manna He sent daily, but they complained and spoke against God; they rebelled.

> Then the Lord sent venomous snakes among them; they bit the people and many Israelites died. The people came to Moses and said, "We sinned when we spoke against the Lord and against you. Pray that the Lord will take the snakes away from us." So Moses prayed for the people.

The Lord said to Moses, "Make a snake and put it up on a pole; anyone who is bitten can look at it and live." So Moses made a bronze snake and put it up on a pole. Then when anyone was bitten by a snake and looked at the bronze snake, he lived. (Numbers 21:6–9)

The pole was a type of the cross. Jesus mentioned it twice referring to His own death on the cross:

Just as Moses lifted up the snake in the desert, so the Son of Man must be lifted up, that everyone who believes in Him may have eternal life. (John 3:14–15)

When Jesus told His disciples the hour had come for His death—in fact, the very reason He came—He said,

Now is the time for judgment on this world; now the prince of this world will be driven out. But I, when I am lifted up from the earth, will draw all men to myself. (John 12:31–32)

When the serpent was lifted up in the wilderness, the people who looked at it were saved from death. As we look at Christ lifted up on the cross, we too will be saved from eternal death and receive everlasting life with Him.

There are no crosses on Mormon buildings, inside or out. The Mormon people have believed Satan's lie that the cross is an evil sign. The truth is: It is a sign of Jesus' victory over Satan.

The All-Sufficient Bread

All men who look to Jesus, believing He is the Bread of Life—just as the manna was for the children of Israel—will have all they need for spiritual life and fellowship with Him eternally:

> Jesus said to them, "I tell you the truth, it is not Moses who has given you the bread from heaven, but it is my Father who gives you the true bread from heaven. For the bread of God is he who comes down from heaven and gives life to the world" (John 6:32–33).

Who Is Jesus, and What Has He Done for Us?

Let's look at some differences:

- Mormon teaching takes salvation out of Jesus' hands. The *hope* is that enough righteous works have been done to achieve the third, or highest, heaven:

  > Some degree of salvation will come to all who have not forfeited their right to it; exaltation is given to those only who by righteous effort have won a claim to God's merciful liberality by which it is bestowed.
  >
  > The Terrestrial Glory . . . These are they who, though honorable, failed to comply with the requirements for exaltation, were blinded by the craftiness of men and unable to receive and obey the higher laws of God.[1]

This quote is by one of the twelve apostles of the Church of Jesus Christ of Latter-day Saints, James Talmage.

- The Bible teaches we are redeemed by the blood of Christ—completely:

  God made him who had no sin to be sin for us, so that in him we might become the righteousness of God. (2 Corinthians 5:21)

- Mormon teaching puts salvation into their own hands:

  For we know that it is by grace that we are saved, after all we can do. (*Book of Mormon*, 2 Nephi 25:23)

- The Bible teaches that our salvation lies in the hands of Jesus—we accept it as the mercy of God. This takes the glory away from us and gives it to God, who provided the way for us:

  For it is by grace you have been saved, through faith—and this not from yourselves, it is the gift of God—not by works, so that no one can boast. (Ephesians 2:8–9)

- Who has the power and authority in the Mormon Church?

  The President of the Church of Jesus Christ of Latter-day Saints holds the keys of salvation for all men now living because he is the only one by whose authorization the sealing power of the priesthood can be used to seal men up to salvation and exaltation in the kingdom of God.[2]

  As pertaining to eternity, priesthood is the eternal power and authority of Deity by which all things exist;

by which they are created, governed, and controlled; by which the universe and worlds without number have come rolling into existence; by which the great plan of creation, redemption, and exaltation operates throughout immensity. It is the power of God.[3]

- Who has the power and authority in Christ's church?

Then Jesus came to them and said, "All authority in heaven and on earth has been given to me" (Matthew 28:18).

Jesus Christ, who has gone into heaven and is at God's right hand with angels, authorities, and powers in submission to Him (1 Peter 3:21–22).

Christ is above every authority, power, dominion, and every title that can be given (see Ephesians 1:20–23).

- How is a person justified in the Mormon Church?

There are some who have striven to obey all the divine commandments, who have accepted the testimony of Christ, obeyed "the laws and ordinances of the [Mormon] gospel," and received the Holy Spirit; these are they who have overcome evil by godly works and who are therefore entitled to the highest glory.[4]

- How is a person justified in Christ's church?

Therefore no one will be declared righteous in his sight by observing the law; rather, through the law we become conscious of sin. But now a righteousness from

God apart from law, has been made known, to which the Law and the Prophets testify. This righteousness from God comes through faith in Jesus Christ to all who believe. There is no difference, for all have sinned and fall short of the glory of God, and are justified freely by his grace through the redemption that came by Christ Jesus. (Romans 3:20–24)

What does the Scripture say? "Abraham believed God, and it was credited to him as righteousness." Now when a man works, his wages are not credited to him as a gift, but as an obligation. However, to the man who does not work but trusts God who justifies the wicked, his faith is credited as righteousness. (Romans 4:3–5)

Since we have now been justified by his blood, how much more shall we be saved from God's wrath through him! For if, when we were God's enemies, we were reconciled to him through the death of his Son, how much more, having been reconciled, shall we be saved through his life. (Romans 5:9–10)

So we are saved, not by how good we are but because we accept Christ's death on the cross as the complete price paid for our sin (see *Mormon Salvation vs. Biblical Salvation* in Glossary).

John Hendee writes in his *Ambassadors for Christ* (Standard Publishing) manual, "We are saved because of our position [in Christ], not our condition!"

Clearly no one is justified before God by the law, because, "The righteous will live by faith" (Galatians 3:11).

Hendee goes on to say, "This conclusion almost always

raises this question: Does this mean it is not important to be good? Of course, the answer found in the Scriptures is no. I must understand the purpose of my freedom."

> You my brothers, were called to be free. But do not use your freedom to indulge the sinful nature; rather, serve one another in love. (Galatians 5:13)

> Live as free men, but do not use your freedom as a cover-up for evil; live as servants of God. (1 Peter 2:16)

> My dear children, I write this to you so that you will not sin. But if anyone does sin, we have one who speaks to the Father in our defense—Jesus Christ, the Righteous One. (1 John 2:1)

"By doing God's will—obeying Him—I am demonstrating my love and appreciation to Him for what He has done for me. In obeying Him, I'm being faithful in advancing His best interests as He is faithful in advancing mine.

"Understanding position and condition changes our new motivation for being good.

"Old motivation—to make me look good. New motivation—to make Him look good."

In Mormonism a person does good things hoping to gain salvation. In Christianity a person does good things out of gratitude for the salvation he already has:

> You are all sons of God through faith in Christ Jesus, for all of you who were baptized into Christ have clothed yourselves with Christ. (Galatians 3:26–27)

How to Run the Race With Jesus

Join a Team

> Therefore, since we are surrounded by such a great cloud of witnesses, let us throw off everything that hinders and the sin that so easily entangles, and let us run with perseverance the race marked out for us. Let us fix our eyes on Jesus, the author and perfecter of our faith, who for the joy set before him endured the cross, scorning its shame, and sat down at the right hand of the throne of God. Consider him who endured such opposition from sinful men, so that you will not grow weary and lose heart. (Hebrews 12:1–3)

In relay races, one runner passes the baton on to another team member until the last runner reaches the finish line. Team up with at least one solid Christian for support during your training period, in addition to church attendance (see appendix B). If possible, join a support group for ex-Mormons.[1]

Ex-Mormon Christians know what it means to have Jesus as their coach. They have followed His training manual—the Bible—and asked Him questions when they were confused.

The process of laying aside the weights of Mormonism is difficult. Let the team members who have already been trained pass the baton on to you. You will find that others who have been through it are empathetic to your plight.

Leaving Mormonism involves four stages, somewhat like the stages of grief after the death of a loved one:

1. Shock and withdrawal

2. Depression

3. Anger

4. Desire to do something about it

The recent ex-Mormon needs much prayer, support, and compassion during these stages.

Many have also expressed fear as a stage that prevents them from moving forward. Fear of shunning from family and friends and/or retribution from Mormon hierarchy sometimes occurs. Some describe an inexplicable dread of leaving the church.

At the moment you ask Jesus into your life, you can put the fear of man behind you forever "because the One who is in you is greater than the one who is in the world" (1 John 4:4).

A recent ex-Mormon who had been haunted by fear was glad to discover this assurance from God's Word: "For God hath not given us a spirit of fear; but of power, and of love, and of a sound mind" (2 Timothy 1:7 KJV).

We can know that when fear grips us we may be viewing

the world through Mormon glasses. Focus on Jesus. He said this:

> So do not be afraid of them. There is nothing concealed that will not be disclosed, or hidden that will not be made known. What I tell you in the dark, speak in the daylight; what is whispered in your ear, proclaim from the roofs. Do not be afraid of those who kill the body but cannot kill the soul.
>
> Rather, be afraid of the One who can destroy both soul and body in hell. Are not two sparrows sold for a penny? Yet not one of them will fall to the ground apart from the will of your Father. And even the very hairs of your head are all numbered. So don't be afraid; you are worth more than many sparrows. (Matthew 10:26–31)

Join Others to Study the Training Manual—the Bible

A discipline I found extremely helpful as I struggled to replace Mormon doctrine with truth from the Bible was a Memorize the Word class. Teaming with at least one other person to repeat my verses weekly freed my mind of "junk food" and replaced it with the "Bread of Life." These verses were food for my hungry soul, and to this day continue in my mind, keeping me spiritually healthy.

Make up a list of verses that are helpful to you; write or type them on 3 x 5 cards. Put them on the mirror in your bathroom to read over daily. Replace negative thoughts with good ones. Paul gives wisdom about our thinking: "Finally, brothers, whatever is true, whatever is noble, whatever is right, whatever is pure, whatever is lovely, whatever is admirable—if anything is excellent or praiseworthy—think about such things" (Philippians 4:8).

A good one to memorize.

Join a Sunday school class or other Christian small group for corporate study of God's Word and fellowship.

Give Your Burdens to the Coach

Most of us don't realize that the load we're trying to run with is slowing us down until we have to sit on the sidelines, unable to continue our race. Jesus said, "Come to me, all you who are weary and burdened, and I will give you rest. Take my yoke upon you and learn from me, for I am gentle and humble in heart, and you will find rest for your souls. For my yoke is easy and my burden is light" (Matthew 11:28–29).

Set aside a time of quiet—just being still and listening—like Mary, who sat at the feet of Jesus. Her sister, Martha, was upset that she didn't help her with meal preparations; but Jesus said about her, "Mary has chosen what is better, and it will not be taken away from her" (Luke 10:38–42).

"Cast all your anxiety on Him because He cares for you" (1 Peter 5:7).

"But those who hope in the Lord will renew their strength. They will soar on wings like eagles; they will run and not grow weary, they will walk and not be faint" (Isaiah 40:31).

Being still before God, waiting and listening for His still, small voice, has been and is for me the most valuable time of my day. It's here that I am renewed, refreshed, equipped for whatever demands my life may hold. It's worth every effort to make that time with Jesus.

Let the Coach Be Coach

It was so hard for me to stop trying to arrange things to suit what I thought was best for everyone. I didn't realize I had taken over some responsibilities that were never mine to begin with. I was trying to be God for my family.

In one of my quiet times, I sensed God telling me, *"You can stop trying to be God now."* It hit me like a hammer blow. I hadn't learned to rely on Him in certain areas of my life. It's a continual process, by the way. A verse that became a favorite was: "Trust in the Lord with all your heart and lean not on your own understanding; in all your ways acknowledge him, and he will make your paths straight" (Proverbs 3:5–6).

I found out His ways are so much better than mine—much higher: "As the heavens are higher than the earth, so are my ways higher than your ways and my thoughts than your thoughts" (Isaiah 55:9).

Thank goodness, God is God and I am not, and never will be. Once I took this big step of letting go and letting God direct the affairs of my life, peace flowed in warm, comforting waves.

Glossary of Mormon Terms

Buildings

Ward: The meetinghouse of the congregation. Several wards (congregations) share one building. Wards meet at different times on Sunday and throughout the week.

Chapel: A designated room within the ward building where the people go on Sunday for *sacrament meetings*.

Temple: A large ostentatious building where baptisms and marriages are performed by proxy for the dead; marriages are "sealed" for "time and all eternity"; and rituals with their signs, covenants, and penalties, called *endowments* are carried out Monday through Saturday.

There are over one hundred temples around the world. Only Mormons in good standing are allowed inside. Most Latter-day Saints marry in a temple, receive their "garments," and never return. Only a small percentage of the eleven million members go to the temple on a regular basis. Once a month each ward has a scheduled time for temple attendance.

Stake House: An administration building (often within a "ward" building) for officers who overlook the affairs of several wards.

Organizational Structure

Priesthood: Latter-day Saints are taught that no one has the authority to officiate in any ordinance—baptism, communion, burial, marriage, etc.—unless he has the priesthood authority administered only through the LDS Church.

All worthy male members of the LDS Church are ordained into the Aaronic priesthood at the age of twelve or older. This "lesser" priesthood is training for the Melchizedek priesthood, or higher priesthood. "As pertaining to man's existence on this earth, priesthood is the power and authority of God delegated to man on earth to act in all things for the salvation of men" (*Gospel Doctrine*, 5th ed., 136–200).

According to Mormon teaching, the priesthood is passed from one having proper authority to a worthy candidate. For instance: Jim was ordained by a high priest, who was ordained by another having authority, and so on through the lineage of Brigham Young, Joseph Smith, Peter, James, and John, and Jesus Christ.

President/Prophet: Also called Seer/Revelator. Presides over the whole church. Considered the liaison between man and God. Two counselors and the president comprise the First Presidency.

Apostles: Members of the Council of the Twelve. They administer the affairs of the LDS Church.

Quorum of Seventy: General authorities of the church. They act under the direction of the Council of the Twelve.

Regional Representative: Men appointed to run the business of a group of stakes combined to form regions or districts. They administer various programs, such as the welfare program, work in the temples, education, banking, insurance, industrial, agricultural, and other business enterprises in which the church has an interest.

Stake President: Presides over the stake (several wards). He is the presiding high priest in the stake and is responsible for and directs all the programs for the church within his stake area.

Bishop: The presiding high priest over a ward. He presides over all ward affairs and members.

Bishopric: Ward bishop and two counselors.

Branch President: Same as the bishop but presides over a congregation of fewer than 500 people. He is assisted by two counselors forming a Branch Presidency and is comparable to a bishopric over a ward.

Relief Society: Organization of adult women. Meet weekly for lessons regarding Mormon doctrine, homemaking skills, and crafts; coordinates with the church welfare system. Oversees visiting teachers who go out in twos calling on women of the church.

Primary: Organization of children, twelve and under.

Missionaries: Young men, nineteen years old, who devote two years; and young women, twenty-one years old, who devote eighteen months away from their own home—many times in foreign countries—to persuade others to become Mormon. Also called *elders* (male) or *sisters* (female).

Deacons: The lowest office in the priesthood hierarchy. They are twelve-year-old, or older, young men. They assist teachers in all their duties, which includes home teaching. They are assigned to pass the sacrament—the bread and water—at sacrament meetings on Sundays; perform messenger service; act as ushers; keep church facilities in good repair; and perform special assignments at the direction of the bishopric.

Other Unique Teachings

Zion: The name by which Mormons identify themselves. "The Church of Jesus Christ of Latter-day Saints is Zion. Joining the Church is becoming a citizen of Zion."[1]

Also referred to as the *New Jerusalem*. Joseph Smith said it was to be built in Jackson County, Missouri (*Doctrine and Covenants*, 84:1–4).

Gospel: When Mormons use the term "gospel," they mean

all the teachings, laws, and ordinances of the Mormon Church. This is *not* the gospel spoken of in the Bible that teaches Jesus made us right with God through His death on the cross (see appendix C; 1 Corinthians 15:1–4; Galatians 1:6–9; Romans 5:8–9; 1 John 1:7–10).

Scriptures: Also called "standard works." These include the *Book of Mormon, Doctrine and Covenants, Pearl of Great Price*, and the Bible. In addition, the words of the prophets and elders of the Mormon Church: "And whatsoever they shall speak when moved upon by the Holy Ghost shall be scripture" (*Doctrine and Covenants*, 68:1–4).

Preexistence: Every human being existed as a spirit child of Heavenly Father before he came to earth to gain a body.

Three Heavens: There are three levels of heaven, or degrees of glory (*Doctrine and Covenants*, 131:1). Those Mormons who have gone through the temple and obeyed all the laws and ordinances of the Mormon gospel will go to the Celestial Kingdom, or highest heaven. From there he/she can progress to the station of a god or goddess. Those who are the good and honorable on earth, but are not Mormon, will go to the Terrestrial Kingdom (*Doctrine and Covenants*, 76:71–80). They have taken the broad way—not the straight and narrow way of Mormonism. The dishonest, liars, sorcerers, adulterers, whoremongers, murderers, and unbelievers will inherit the Telestial Kingdom, or lowest heaven (*Doctrine and Covenants*, 76:81–113).

Family Exaltation and Genealogy: For family members or

anyone who has died without accepting Mormonism, accurate genealogy records must be submitted to church headquarters in Salt Lake City, Utah. The dead person's name can be taken into the temple and necessary works performed for them by proxy. They are baptized into the Mormon Church or married for time and all eternity—all vicariously. Mormons perform for the dead the same rituals they went through the first time they went to the temple.

Gathering of Israel: It is the Mormon's belief that Heavenly Father's chosen people, his covenant family, are known as *Israel*. They believe they are the true Jewish people. Members of the Church of Jesus Christ of Latter-day Saints are members of the covenant family and have the responsibility of being examples to the world. Drawing people to the Mormon Church is called the gathering of Israel. Also known as the . . .

Friendshiping Program: Being kind to non-member neighbors. Taking fresh bread or a meal to their home on special occasions, etc.

Family Home Preparedness: Better known as "a year's supply." The president of the Mormon Church in 1937 instructed the saints: "Let every head of every household see to it that he has on hand enough food, clothing, and, where possible, fuel for at least a year ahead" (*Conference Report*, April 1937, 26). Mormons are known for their well-stocked, walk-in-style pantries. A two-year supply is now recommended.

Word of Wisdom: Abstinence from coffee, tea, alcohol, and tobacco. Obeying the Word of Wisdom is used as a measuring rod to determine in part the personal worthiness of church members (*Doctrine and Covenants*, 89).

Family Home Evening: A Monday night set aside to stay at home with the family. They do something special together: play games, have a lesson. Father takes charge.

Seminary: In areas highly populated with Mormons, junior and senior high schools have Mormon Church-owned-and-operated seminary buildings across the street from the schools. Mormon students are granted release time for religious studies. A paid seminary professor teaches LDS doctrine.

CTR Rings: When LDS children reach the age of eight, they are instructed that this is the age of "accountability" and they should be baptized into the Mormon Church at that time. They are given a ring with the letters: C-T-R, "choose the right," reminding them to make the right decision.

Terminology Differences

Many say, "I know my Mormon friend is a Christian. She says she has accepted Jesus as her Savior." Because Mormons use the same words for salvation that Christians do, we may think they *are* Christian. It's very important, however, to understand the thinking behind the terms.

Mormon Savior: Christ's death and resurrection guarantee our physical resurrection from the dead—only. Where our spirits go is determined by our efforts here on earth. For example: Have we done enough good works? Have we repented enough?

Biblical Savior: Christ died to pay our debt of sin so we could have eternal life with Him. He saved us from spiritual death and an eternity apart from Him. Our part is to acknowledge and accept His death as the full, complete, and final payment for our sinful nature. We should have been on the cross, but He took our place. We can never do enough good works or repent enough to be worthy of this gift of mercy.

Mormon Heavenly Father: A god-man and our biological father who, with one of many heavenly mothers, conceived us as a spirit baby in a pre-Earth life. Every human being that ever existed, or will exist, first lived in preexistence with a flesh-and-bone heavenly father and a mother before our parents on Earth chose us and brought us down to Earth and gave us a physical body.

Biblical Heavenly Father: The immortal, invisible, unchangeable God, who is Spirit.

Mormon Salvation: Universal resurrection from the grave. Man determines where he will spend eternity by how good he is. He must earn his place in heaven.

Biblical Salvation: Man's fate is determined by his belief in Jesus—either eternal damnation or eternal life with Christ (see John 3:16–18).

Endnotes

Chapter 4

1. Will L. Thompson, "The World Has Need of Willing Men," *Hymns of The Church of Jesus Christ of Latter-day Saints* (Salt Lake City: Deseret News Press, 1948), 206.

Chapter 5

1. William Fowler, "We Thank Thee, O God, for a Prophet"; William Clayton, "Come, Come, Ye Saints"; and Eliza Snow, "O My Father," *Hymns of the Church*, 196, 13, 138.

Chapter 8

1. All quotations of the Mormon temple ceremony are taken from Chuck Sackett's 1982 book *What's Going On*

in There? Used with permission. The wording is taken from the transcription of a pocket tape recorder carried by one of the patrons inside the Los Angeles temple during the actual endowment ceremony. The ceremonies have been verified by comparing them with copies of temple worker instruction books or similar authentic sources.

Chapter 9

1. On April 10, 1990, changes were made in the Mormon temple ceremony rituals. These changes reflect objections by non-Mormons and liberal Mormon critics. The signs of the death oaths have been eliminated, though the oath itself is still repeated. The woman's oath of obedience to her husband is also cut from the ceremony, as well as the portrayal of Christian pastors as paid agents of Satan.

Chapter 10

1. The words *pay lay ale* (another possible translation of *pele heylel* in Hebrew is "wonderful Lucifer," *Strong's Concordance*, Hebrew dictionary, item #6382 amd 1966) have been stricken from the Mormon temple ceremony as of April 1990. Only the interpreted words, "O God, hear the words of my mouth," remain. A man depicting Lucifer answers this prayer of Adam in the Creation room.

Chapter 16

1. Eliza Snow, "O My Father"; William W. Phelps, "Praise to the Man," *Hymns of the Church*, 138, 326.

Chapter 21

1. Bruce R. McConkie, *Mormon Doctrine* (Salt Lake City: Bookcraft, Inc., 1966), 576–77.

Appendix A

1. Joseph Smith, *Doctrines of Salvation* (Salt Lake City: Bookcraft, Inc., 1954), 1:135.
2. See *Witness to Mormons* (Phoenix: Concerned Christians, 1983), 9, 12–13, for additional information.
3. Ibid., 20.
4. Walter Martin, *The Kingdom of the Cults* (Minneapolis: Bethany House Publishers, 1997 [revised edition]), 23.
5. See *Witness to Mormons*, 28.
6. *History of the Church* (Salt Lake City: Deseret Book Company, 1950), 6:408–09.
7. Josh McDowell and Don Stewart, *Understanding the Cults* (San Bernardino: Here's Life Publishers, Inc., Campus Crusade for Christ, Inc., 1982), 21.
8. Joseph Fielding Smith, *Teaching of the Prophet Joseph Smith* (Salt Lake City: Deseret Book Company, 1976), 194.
9. Milton R. Hunter, *Gospel Through the Ages* (Salt Lake City: Deseret Book Company, 1958), 15.

10. McConkie, *Mormon Doctrine*, 590.

11. McDowell and Stewart, *Understanding the Cults*, 24.

Appendix B

1. If more evidence is needed, read Fawn Brodie, *No Man Knows My History: The Life of Joseph Smith* (New York: Alfred A. Knopf Publisher, 1982); Stanley P. Hirshson, *Lion of the Lord: A Biography of Brigham Young* (New York: Alfred A. Knopf Publisher, 1973); Thelma Geer, *Mama, Mormonism, and Me* (Chicago: Moody Press, 1986).

2. Marvin W. Cowen, *Mormon Claims Answered* (Salt Lake City: Utah Christian Publications, 1989); Harry L. Ropp, *Are the Mormon Scriptures Reliable?* (Downers Grove, Ill.: InterVarsity Press), released in 1995 under the title: *Is Mormonism Christian? A Look at the Teachings of the Mormon Religion* (Joplin, Mo.: College Press Publishing Co., Inc.); Floyd McElveen, *God's Word, Final, Infallible, and Forever* (Grand Rapids, Mich.: Gospel Truth Ministries, 1985). Most of these titles can be obtained through Concerned Christians or any Christian bookstore.

3. Read *Witness to Mormons*. An additional reading list is available through the Concerned Christians office. The most valuable book of all is, of course, the Bible.

Appendix C

1. James Talmage, *Articles of Faith* (Salt Lake City: Deseret Book Company, 1976), 91–92.

2. McConkie, *Mormon Doctrine*, 411.
3. Ibid., 594.
4. Talmage, *Articles of Faith*, 91–92.

Appendix D

1. If you don't know of a Christian ex-Mormon group near you, write: Concerned Christians, P.O. Box 18, Mesa, AZ 85211. We will try to locate a support group for you.

Glossary

1. McConkie, *Mormon Doctrine*, 854.

Build a Strong Foundation

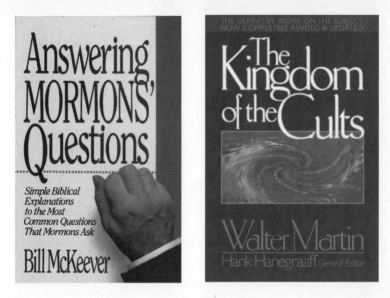

Thank you for selecting a book from
BETHANY HOUSE PUBLISHERS

Bethany House Publishers is a ministry of Bethany Fellowship International, an interdenominational, nonprofit organization committed to spreading the Good News of Jesus Christ around the world through evangelism, church planting, literature distribution, and care for those in need. Missionary training is offered through Bethany College of Missions.

Bethany Fellowship International is a member of the National Association of Evangelicals and subscribes to its statement of faith. If you would like further information, please contact:

Bethany Fellowship International
6820 Auto Club Road
Bloomington, MN 55438 USA